P9-CRN-669

Picnics and Barbecues

Picnics and Barbecues

Myra Street

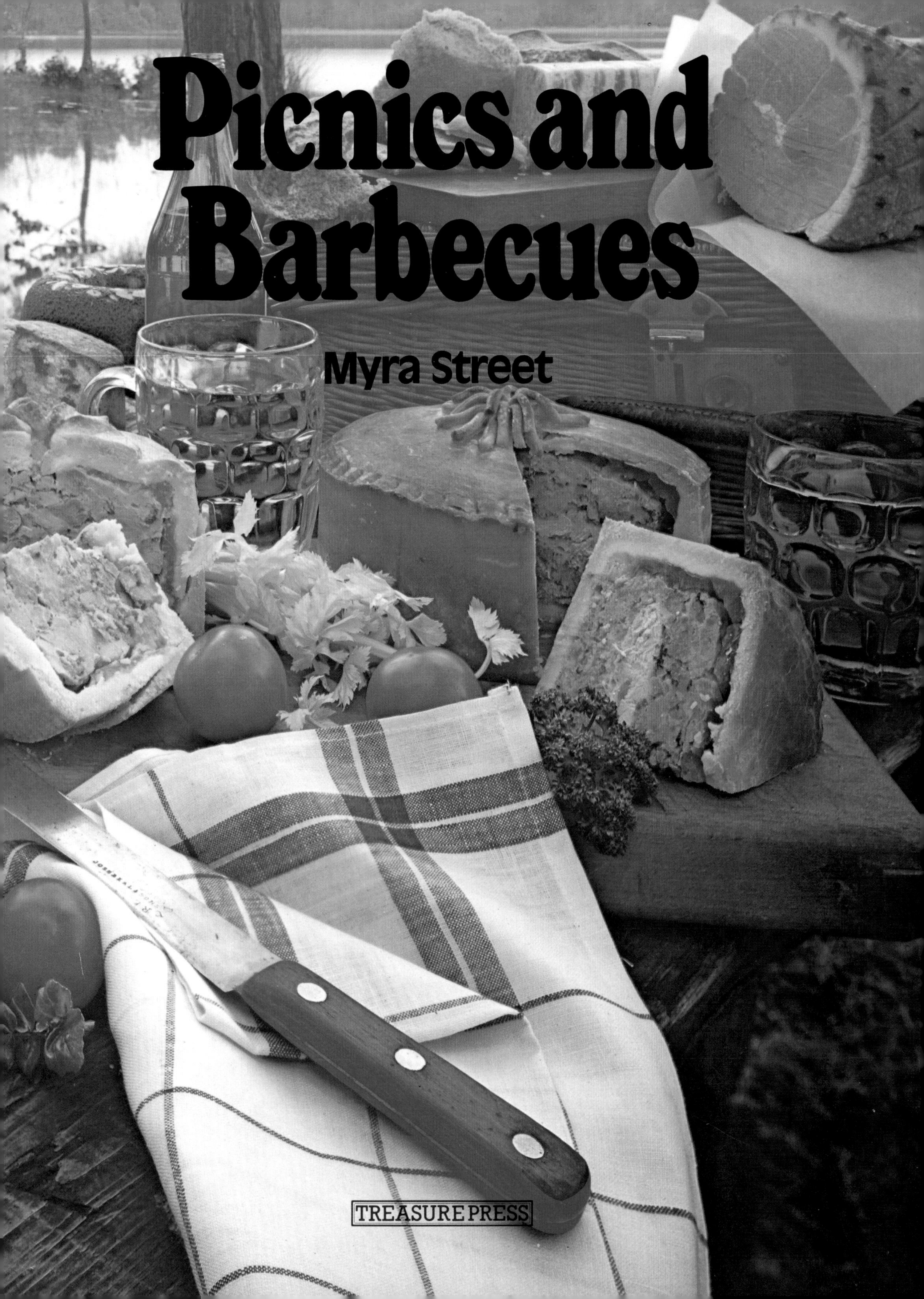

TREASURE PRESS

Contents

First published in Great Britain by Sundial Books Ltd
This edition published by Treasure Press
59 Grosvenor Street
London W1

Reprinted 1985
ISBN 0 907407 91 9
Printed in Hong Kong

Barbecues

On a fine summer's day there is nothing to equal the aroma of food cooking over charcoal out of doors. Barbecues, cook-outs and picnics have become increasingly popular as many more people like to spend their leisure time outside.

Whether you have a large garden, a small patio or just a balcony you can join the barbecue enthusiasts, as there is equipment available for every space and every purse. The fun of barbecueing has great appeal for all the family, and with a little preparation beforehand, it can become a way of life in fine weather.

Siting the barbecue

A permanent barbecue should be built on a site which will not disturb the neighbours, as some smoke and cooking smells are inevitable. Portable barbecues can be sited to suit the wind on any particular day.

Size of barbecue

Whether you are building or buying a barbecue you must ensure that its cooking area is large enough for your needs. An area of about 45 cm (18 inches) across is sufficient space to cook food for eight people. But it is as well to make provision for a smaller fire area if you are catering for fewer. This is easily done by temporarily bricking off the larger area on a permanent barbecue to concentrate the fire on a smaller one.

Charcoal is not cheap, so it is as well to take advantage of all the heat and avoid waste. Remember, too, that the meat used for barbecueing is generally expensive as it must be of the best quality.

Barbecues

Charcoal chips or briquettes are the best fuel for the barbecue, but you must allow enough time for the fire to reach a good cooking heat. Do not use branded firelighters or dangerous liquids such as paraffin or petrol as they can all taint the food and might flare up.

To light the fire use paper and dry sticks, or special solid fuel tablets (available from chemists) which start charcoal burning easily. Begin by making a flat bed of charcoal on top of the paper and sticks, extending about 2.5 cm (1 inch) beyond the cooking area. Then push the coals into a pyramid shape to allow the air to circulate and set them alight.

Time your eating to suit the fire: charcoal chips will need 45 to 60 minutes; briquettes 30 to 40 minutes. In daylight the coals will turn

DRY DUBONNET
GAUCHO
GRILL

grey with ash; they only glow in the dark. You can test the temperature of the fire by very cautiously holding the palm of your hand about 7.5 cm (3 inches) above the grid. If you can stand the heat for 2 to 3 seconds it indicates a hot fire; 4 seconds a medium hot fire; 5 seconds a low fire. Push the pyramid down with tongs or sticks before you start to cook. The cooking heat can be varied by adjusting the distance between the grid and the fire; and then adjusting the distance between the food and the hottest, central part of the fire. If the fire is not hot enough food will cook unevenly and become dry.

Should the fire not be entirely burnt out when cooking is finished, dowse the charcoal with a little water and save it for when you are building the next one.

Barbecue equipment

Long-handled fork, spoon and fish slice

Tongs for handling food and coals (two pairs are better than one)

Long-handled brush for basting (a new paint brush is suitable)

Plastic sprinkler bottle to dowse flames when food flares from dripping fat (do not use a bottle that previously contained inflammable liquids), or a water pistol

Foil

A hinged wire grill (useful for food which breaks up easily, such as fish or hamburgers)

A flat baking sheet

Skewers

Oven gloves

Apron

Damp cloth

Absorbent kitchen paper

A table placed beside the barbecue can hold food, marinades and equipment.

Cooking and serving tips

Place the barbecue away from the house, trees, dry grass or shrubs.

Although you will need a draught for the fire, it is better not to be smoked out before you eat.

Prepare sauces, marinades, relishes and salads well in advance.

When catering for large numbers it is easier to cheat a little and part-cook items such as large joints of beef or lamb before the party; keep the food refrigerated until required. This is better than keeping guests waiting for hours before being fed.

To give a pleasant aroma to barbecued food burn a few sprigs of fresh herbs in the charcoal while the food is cooking. Rosemary, marjoram or thyme are very aromatic.

Brush the grid with oil from time to time to prevent food sticking.

Allow plenty of food; eating outdoors creates hearty appetites.

French bread and vegetables to accompany meats can be wrapped in foil and heated on the side of the barbecue.

Skewered vegetables are easiest to eat out of doors.

Score the fat of chops and steaks to prevent them from curling.

Provide paper napkins, and some finger bowls, as eating outside can become messy.

Care of the barbecue

Keep portable metal barbecues under cover when not in use or they will rust. Cover brick barbecues to keep out rainwater and remove metal parts. A dustbin lid will do, but make sure it is securely anchored or it may blow away and cause damage. Scrape down and clean the grid frequently for best results.

Rôtisserie or spit cooking

A battery-operated rôtisserie will give excellent results with joints of beef and lamb, chickens and ducks. Ensure that the spit is inserted centrally through the joint or bird, otherwise the strain on the motor will eventually force it to stop, or it will turn unevenly and the food will cook unevenly.

It is vital that the fire is hot enough; a 2–3 kg (4–5 lb) roast will require about 2.5 kg (5 lb) of charcoal to cook.

Beef and lamb may be left pink, but a meat thermometer is really the safest way of ensuring that large pieces of meat and poultry are sufficiently cooked.

Always use a drip pan to catch drips from the roast. Make this by cutting a double thickness of foil 5 cm (2 inches) longer than the roast. Fold around a rectangular object such as a book, making a dish about 15 cm (6 inches) wide and 3 cm (1¼ inches) deep. This will prevent fat from flaring up on the fire.

Vegetables can always be cooked on the grid underneath the joint towards the end of the cooking time.

Building a barbecue

There is no need to spend a great deal of money for a good permanent barbecue. You can build the one shown here with a minimum of expertise and 36 bricks.

First level the ground to make a good flat base about 60 × 90 cm (2 × 3 feet). Lay the first row two bricks deep on each side, with two bricks at the back between the sides. Use an ordinary mortar mix for building. For the second row place three bricks along the back and one and a half along the sides. Continue with this alternating pattern for four rows. With the third row you could insert a long plank as shown in the drawing. This is not essential, but very useful for putting down basting sauces, marinades and cooking utensils. To insert the plank, you will have to chip a piece from the half bricks.

On top of the fourth row place a large slab of real stone or slate (not concrete or reconstituted stone as this can explode when hot) about 60 × 90 cm (2 × 3 feet). Your local garden centre or builders' merchant should be able to provide this. Finish off on top of the slab with two more rows of bricks. Place a fire basket on the centre of the slab; never light a fire directly on it as it will crack in the heat. Finally, put an ordinary oven shelf or metal bars on top of the final row of bricks.

For the fire it is best to use charcoal, either in briquettes or random pieces. Charcoal is much more satisfactory than such things as wood, because it provides good heat without flaming and burning the food.

You may find that the grill shelf is too close to the fire for some types of food; in this case lay another row of bricks, without mortar so they can be moved to suit the food being cooked.

This barbecue is comfortable to use if you are of average height. For extra height add another row of bricks at the base, using 42 instead of 36.

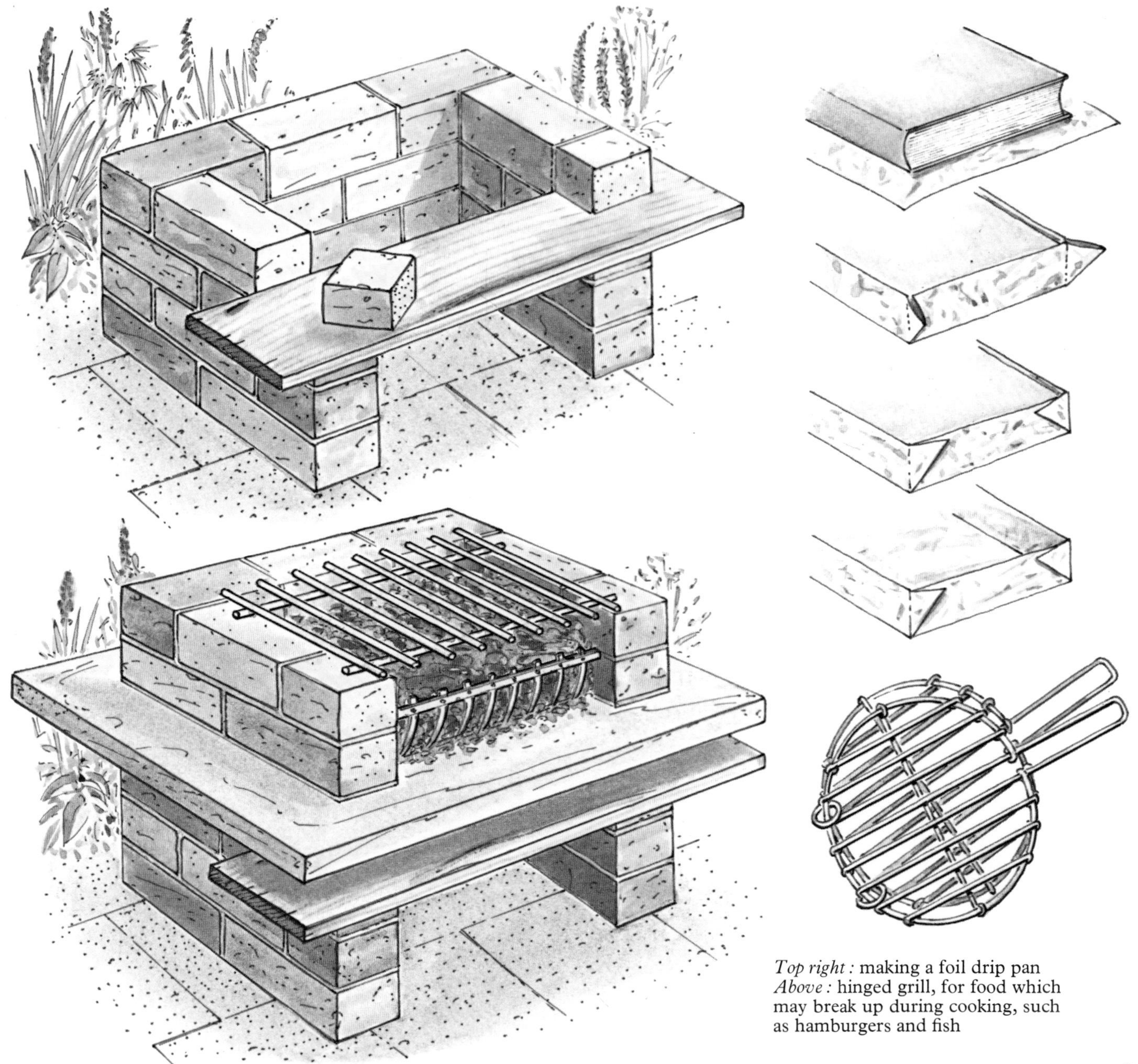

Top right: making a foil drip pan
Above: hinged grill, for food which may break up during cooking, such as hamburgers and fish

Picnics

In pleasant weather, a picnic meal is ideal because it enables you to take full advantage of the sunshine. But even on those occasions when you set off, with well-stocked hamper, into the country and it pours with rain, you can still enjoy your picnic – in the car.

Picnics once were extremely grand, with servants appearing at the appointed hour and place to unpack the food, the silver cutlery, china and glass, and serve the assembled company. Today most of us do the work ourselves. But if the family likes picnics, then the preparation can be shared so that everyone enjoys the outing.

With all the modern picnic equipment available, at reasonable cost, there need never be wilted lettuce or a dried-up sandwich. Regular picnickers will find an insulated bag or box a great advantage, as this ensures that the food and drinks arrive fresh. A cold brick or bag inside the insulated bag will keep everything icy cold and crisp. These cold bricks or bags are first frozen solid in the freezing compartment of the refrigerator or freezer, and can be used over and over again unless they are pierced and the freezing fluid leaks out. (Insulated bags and bricks will also transport frozen food from shop to home in good condition.)

Elaborate picnic sets are useful and compact. They do tend to be expensive, but it is simple to provide inexpensive alternatives. Any basket, canvas or plastic bag can be used, with unbreakable plates and cups and a set of picnic cutlery, which can be throwouts from the kitchen or plastic. For those who do not want to take the washing-up home there are attractively designed paper plates and cups, but these are expensive for regular picnics. Plastic tablecloths are useful too, making good 'tables' if laid on a flat surface, and they are easy to clean.

A picnic can range from a three-course meal with pâté, cold meats or pies with salads, then a sweet followed by fruit and cheese, to the simple soup and sandwich type. The more elaborate the picnic the more baggage you will need, and it is wise to keep this in mind when choosing a site. An inaccessible cove may be lovely to visit, but climbing up and down rocks with seats and bags on a hot day is not amusing. Many beauty spots have picnic areas near the car parks, and this makes catering easy. But do remember to clear away all your rubbish, otherwise beautiful countryside soon becomes a rubbish dump, and beaches and woodland can be hazardous if littered with broken glass and jagged cans.

Cooking out of doors at picnics is great fun and a small portable barbecue or Hibachi grill can be stowed in the boot of the car and used to cook sausages, bacon, chops, hamburgers and skewered meat, or fresh fish when you can buy it at the seaside. Great care must be taken to extinguish fires or hot coals properly to ensure that your picnic site does not become a fire hazard.

A well-chilled bottle of wine or beer to complete the meal is splendid, but not if you have forgotten to take the opener; the best way of avoiding such minor disasters is to make a check list before you go.

Picnic check list

Freezer bag or insulated box
Cold bricks or bags
3-in-1 corkscrew, bottle and tin opener
Picnic bag with cups, plates, cutlery, etc.
Sharp knife in protective casing
Salt and pepper
Plastic bags for rubbish
Vacuum flasks or wide jug for hot or cold drinks or soup
Foil or plastic film for protecting food from flies and insects
Insect repellent
Working torch for returning home late
First-aid kit equipped to deal with stings, burns and cuts
Damp cloth or sponge in plastic bag, plus towel

Handy food tips

Unpeeled eggs and small fruits such as greengages and plums can be safely carried in egg cartons.
Rolled slices of meat can be easily eaten from wooden cocktail sticks.
Small plastic bottles or tubes with good top seals, or screw-on caps, thoroughly washed, can be used for carrying salad dressings, mustard, etc.
Undiluted fruit squashes can be packed with ice cubes in a wide-mouthed bottle to provide well-chilled drinks on arrival.
Several thin slices of meat are easier to eat than one thick slice in sandwiches.

MARINADES AND SAUCES

Although marinades and sauces have different functions they are also to some extent interchangeable. As barbecued food is cooked fairly rapidly over hot coals it must be tender to be successful, hence the frequent use of marinades for meat. A marinade is usually based on vinegar, wine or lemon juice, and it is the acid in these which tenderizes the meat. At the same time butter or oil add moisture and herbs, spices and seasonings add extra flavour.

Food can either be brushed with a marinade and then placed in a suitable dish with the remainder, or put in a polythene freezer bag. This is a very good way of marinating as you can make sure the marinade reaches all parts of the meat simply by turning the bag over. If food is to be marinated for a long time it is best to put it in the refrigerator; but for a short time this is unnecessary. Whenever marinated food has been in the refrigerator it should be brought back to room temperature before cooking, otherwise the cooking time given will be insufficient.

To baste food simply means brushing on a marinade, sauce or oil during the cooking. This helps to keep the food moist, while at the same time giving it a crisp, well-flavoured exterior. A large pastry brush or a new paint brush is ideal for basting. Usually basting should be done towards the end of cooking to prevent the food tasting only of the basting mixture or becoming charred and bitter on the outside. Food is often marinated and then basted with the remaining marinade.

Sauces are served with barbecued food to complement its crispness, and they too can be used to baste the food during cooking. Keep sauces hot on the edge of the barbecue in a flameproof dish or small saucepan.

Tenderizing marinade

Metric	*Imperial*
150 ml malt or wine vinegar	*¼ pint malt or wine vinegar*
150 ml water	*¼ pint water*
1 large onion, peeled and sliced	*1 large onion, peeled and sliced*
6 cloves	*6 cloves*
2 bay leaves	*2 bay leaves*
6 black peppercorns, slightly crushed	*6 black peppercorns, slightly crushed*
1 × 5 ml spoon salt	*1 teaspoon salt*

Mix all the ingredients together and leave for at least 12 hours. Use for tenderizing tougher cuts of meat such as rib joints, top rump, breast of lamb and spare ribs, by allowing them to stand in the mixture for 24 to 36 hours in the refrigerator. For steaks, chops and skewered food 1 to 5 hours is sufficient.
Makes about 300 ml (½ pint)

Oriental marinade

Metric	*Imperial*
4 × 15 ml spoons soy sauce	*4 tablespoons soy sauce*
2 × 15 ml spoons clear honey	*2 tablespoons clear honey*
4 × 15 ml spoons sherry	*4 tablespoons sherry*
1 × 5 ml spoon ground cinnamon	*1 teaspoon ground cinnamon*
Large pinch of pepper	*Large pinch of pepper*
1 × 2.5 ml spoon ground cloves	*½ teaspoon ground cloves*
4 × 15 ml spoons cold tea	*4 tablespoons cold tea*
1 garlic clove, crushed	*1 garlic clove, crushed*

Mix the ingredients together and cover the food, either in a dish or in a new polythene bag. This marinade is suitable for most meats, especially pork or beef. Marinate small pieces of food for several hours and larger pieces for 8 to 24 hours in the refrigerator. The marinade may then be used to baste the food while cooking for a crisp brown appearance.
Makes about 250 ml (8 fl oz)

Tenderizing marinade on a beef kebab

Honey basting sauce

Metric	*Imperial*
2 × 15 ml spoons oil	*2 tablespoons oil*
1 onion, peeled and finely chopped	*1 onion, peeled and finely chopped*
1 garlic clove, crushed	*1 garlic clove, crushed*
4 × 15 ml spoons orange juice	*4 tablespoons orange juice*
2 × 15 ml spoons clear honey	*2 tablespoons clear honey*
3 × 15 ml spoons wine vinegar	*3 tablespoons wine vinegar*
1 × 15 ml spoon Worcestershire sauce	*1 tablespoon Worcestershire sauce*
1 × 5 ml spoon horseradish sauce	*1 teaspoon horseradish sauce*
1 × 5 ml spoon dry mustard	*1 teaspoon dry mustard*
Salt	*Salt*
Freshly ground pepper	*Freshly ground pepper*
Large pinch of dried rosemary	*Large pinch of dried rosemary*
Large pinch of dried thyme	*Large pinch of dried thyme*

Cooking Time: 10 minutes

Heat the oil in a saucepan and add the onion and garlic. Cook until soft but not brown. Stir in the remaining ingredients with salt and pepper to taste and simmer for 5 minutes. Allow to cool if using as a marinade (leave for 4 to 6 hours in the refrigerator), or use immediately as a basting sauce for poultry, spare ribs or breast of lamb.

Makes a generous 150 ml (¼ pint)

Soured cream marinade

Metric	*Imperial*
1 × 150 ml carton soured cream	*1 × 5 fl oz carton soured cream*
1 × 15 ml spoon lemon juice	*1 tablespoon lemon juice*
1 garlic clove, crushed	*1 garlic clove, crushed*
Salt	*Salt*
Freshly ground pepper	*Freshly ground pepper*
1 celery stalk, thinly sliced	*1 celery stalk, thinly sliced*
Large pinch of paprika	*Large pinch of paprika*
1 × 2.5 ml spoon Worcestershire sauce	*½ teaspoon Worcestershire sauce*

Put the soured cream in a bowl and add the lemon juice, garlic and salt and pepper to taste. Mix well. Stir in the celery, paprika and Worcestershire sauce. Use this marinade for steak, lamb chops, chicken portions and skewered food, allowing 2 to 4 hours depending on size of meat.

Makes about 150 ml (¼ pint)

Red wine barbecue marinade

Metric	*Imperial*
150 ml red wine	*¼ pint red wine*
2 × 15 ml spoons lemon juice	*2 tablespoons lemon juice*
1 onion, peeled and sliced	*1 onion, peeled and sliced*
1 carrot, peeled and sliced	*1 carrot, peeled and sliced*
1 celery stalk, chopped	*1 celery stalk, chopped*
1 fresh parsley sprig or 1 × 2.5 ml spoon dried parsley	*1 fresh parsley sprig or ½ teaspoon dried parsley*
1 fresh thyme sprig or 1 × 2.5 ml spoon dried thyme	*1 fresh thyme sprig or ½ teaspoon dried thyme*
1 bay leaf	*1 bay leaf*
6 black peppercorns, slightly crushed	*6 black peppercorns, slightly crushed*
2–4 × 15 ml spoons oil	*2–4 tablespoons oil*

Mix all the ingredients together and allow to stand for about 1 hour before using. (Add the oil only if the marinade is to be used for lean meat such as chicken, turkey or venison.) Marinate poultry for 2 to 4 hours; skewered meat 1 to 2 hours; large joints up to 12 hours in the refrigerator. The marinade can be used as a sauce afterwards to avoid wasting the wine.

Makes about 300 ml (½ pint)

Variation:

White wine may be substituted for red to marinate veal, pork, poultry or fish.

Soured cream marinade; Honey basting sauce; White wine barbecue marinade (on fish)

Hollandaise sauce

Metric	*Imperial*
2 × 15 ml spoons water	*2 tablespoons water*
6 peppercorns, slightly crushed	*6 peppercorns, slightly crushed*
1 × 15 ml spoon tarragon vinegar	*1 tablespoon tarragon vinegar*
2 egg yolks	*2 egg yolks*
125 g butter	*4 oz butter*
Pinch of salt	*Pinch of salt*
Few drops of lemon juice	*Few drops of lemon juice*

Cooking Time: About 10 to 15 minutes

Put the water, peppercorns and vinegar in a saucepan and bring to the boil. Boil until the liquid has reduced by half. Place the egg yolks in the top of a double boiler, or in a heatproof bowl over a saucepan of hot water (do not allow the bowl to touch the water). Add the strained vinegar mixture. Whisk over a moderate heat, adding the butter in small pieces. The mixture will start to thicken but will do so mainly on the bottom of the bowl if not continually whisked. Remove from the heat just before it is thick as the sauce will continue to cook in the bowl. Taste and adjust the seasoning; flavour with lemon juice.

Serve with fish.

Makes a generous 150 ml (¼ pint)

Béarnaise sauce

Metric	*Imperial*
2 × 5 ml spoons chopped fresh tarragon or *1 × 5 ml spoon dried tarragon*	*2 teaspoons chopped fresh tarragon* or *1 teaspoon dried tarragon*
2 × 5 ml spoons chopped spring onions	*2 teaspoons chopped spring onions*
Salt	*Salt*
Freshly ground pepper	*Freshly ground pepper*
3 × 15 ml spoons wine vinegar	*3 tablespoons wine vinegar*
150 ml Hollandaise sauce	*¼ pint Hollandaise sauce*

Put the tarragon, spring onions, salt and pepper to taste and the wine vinegar in a saucepan. Bring to the boil and boil until reduced to a glaze. Stir into the Hollandaise sauce. (Do not allow the sauce to thicken too much before adding the glaze.)

Serve with steak, skewered beef or hamburgers.

Béarnaise sauce; Hollandaise sauce

Lemon marinade

Metric	*Imperial*
6 × 15 ml spoons lemon juice	*6 tablespoons lemon juice*
Salt	*Salt*
Freshly ground pepper	*Freshly ground pepper*
Large pinch of paprika	*Large pinch of paprika*
2 × 15 ml spoons oil	*2 tablespoons oil*
1 bay leaf	*1 bay leaf*
1 fresh parsley sprig	*1 fresh parsley sprig*
1 small onion, peeled and sliced (optional)	*1 small onion, peeled and sliced (optional)*

Mix all the ingredients together with salt and pepper to taste in a screw-topped jar and shake well. Use to marinate fish for 1 to 2 hours in the refrigerator before cooking. Baste towards the end of the cooking time with the marinade.
Makes scant 150 ml (¼ pint)

Armenian marinade

Metric	*Imperial*
4 × 15 ml spoons oil	*4 tablespoons oil*
2 × 15 ml spoons lemon juice	*2 tablespoons lemon juice*
1 × 2.5 ml spoon dried marjoram	*½ teaspoon dried marjoram*
1 × 2.5 ml spoon dried thyme	*½ teaspoon dried thyme*
Salt	*Salt*
Freshly ground pepper	*Freshly ground pepper*
1 garlic clove, crushed	*1 garlic clove, crushed*
1 onion, peeled and finely chopped	*1 onion, peeled and finely chopped*
2 × 15 ml spoons chopped fresh parsley	*2 tablespoons chopped fresh parsley*

Mix all the ingredients together with salt and pepper to taste in a screw-topped jar or in a bowl. Use this marinade for lamb chops, skewered lamb, chicken and turkey pieces, leaving for 2 to 4 hours in the refrigerator.
Makes scant 150 ml (¼ pint)

Lemon marinade (on fish); Armenian marinade

Smoky barbecue sauce (and on meat); Tomato sauce; Creole sauce

Creole sauce

Metric	*Imperial*
2 × 15 ml spoons oil	*2 tablespoons oil*
1 large onion, peeled and finely chopped	*1 large onion, peeled and finely chopped*
1 green pepper, cored, seeded and finely chopped	*1 green pepper, cored, seeded and finely chopped*
1 × 400 g can tomatoes	*1 × 14 oz can tomatoes*
1 small can red pimientos, drained and chopped	*1 small can red pimientos, drained and chopped*
1 × 5 ml spoon sugar	*1 teaspoon sugar*
Large pinch of dry mustard	*Large pinch of dry mustard*
Pinch of chilli powder (optional)	*Pinch of chilli powder (optional)*
1 × 15 ml spoon lemon juice	*1 tablespoon lemon juice*
Salt	*Salt*
Freshly ground pepper	*Freshly ground pepper*
1 × 15 ml spoon chopped fresh parsley	*1 tablespoon chopped fresh parsley*

Cooking Time: About 25 minutes

Heat the oil in a saucepan and add the onion and green pepper. Cook until the onion is soft but not brown. Add the tomatoes, with the can juice, breaking them down with a wooden spoon, the pimientos, sugar, mustard, chilli powder, if using, lemon juice and salt and pepper to taste. Stir well and bring to the boil. Simmer for 20 minutes. Stir in the chopped parsley before serving.
Serve with fish or skewered food.
Makes scant 150 ml (¼ pint)

Tomato sauce

Metric	Imperial
2 × 15 ml spoons oil	*2 tablespoons oil*
2 onions, peeled and finely diced	*2 onions, peeled and finely diced*
1 garlic clove, crushed	*1 garlic clove, crushed*
1 celery stalk, chopped	*1 celery stalk, chopped*
1 carrot, peeled and diced	*1 carrot, peeled and diced*
1 kg tomatoes or 2 × 400 g cans tomatoes	*2 lb tomatoes or 2 × 14 oz cans tomatoes*
1 × 5 ml spoon dried oregano or 2 fresh oregano sprigs	*1 teaspoon dried oregano or 2 fresh oregano sprigs*
1 bay leaf	*1 bay leaf*
1 fresh parsley sprig	*1 fresh parsley sprig*
600 ml chicken or beef stock	*1 pint chicken or beef stock*
2 × 15 ml spoons red wine (optional)	*2 tablespoons red wine (optional)*
2 × 15 ml spoons tomato purée	*2 tablespoons tomato purée*
1 × 5 ml spoon Worcestershire sauce	*1 teaspoon Worcestershire sauce*
Salt	*Salt*
Freshly ground black pepper	*Freshly ground black pepper*

Cooking Time: 50 minutes

Heat the oil in a saucepan and add the onions, garlic, celery and carrot. Allow to cook gently until soft but not brown. Stir in the tomatoes (with the can juice if using canned tomatoes), and break them down with a wooden spoon. Stir in the remaining ingredients with salt and pepper to taste. Bring to the boil and simmer gently for 45 minutes. Strain the sauce if fresh tomatoes with skins have been used, or liquidize if a smooth sauce is required. Many people enjoy little chunks of vegetable in the sauce and if this is the case then do not strain. The sauce should be reduced to the correct consistency by simmering, and does not need thickening agents. Taste and adjust seasoning.

Makes about 600 ml (1 pint)

Smoky barbecue sauce

Metric	Imperial
25 g butter	*1 oz butter*
1 onion, peeled and finely chopped	*1 onion, peeled and finely chopped*
1 garlic clove, crushed	*1 garlic clove, crushed*
2 × 15 ml spoons wine vinegar	*2 tablespoons wine vinegar*
150 ml water or stock	*¼ pint water or stock*
1 × 15 ml spoon prepared English mustard	*1 tablespoon prepared English mustard*
2 × 15 ml spoons demerara sugar	*2 tablespoons demerara sugar*
1 slice of lemon	*1 slice of lemon*
1 bay leaf	*1 bay leaf*
Pinch of cayenne pepper	*Pinch of cayenne pepper*
2 × 15 ml spoons Worcestershire sauce	*2 tablespoons Worcestershire sauce*
6 × 15 ml spoons tomato ketchup or Tomato Sauce (see above)	*6 tablespoons tomato ketchup or Tomato Sauce (see above)*
2 × 15 ml spoons tomato purée	*2 tablespoons tomato purée*
Salt	*Salt*
Freshly ground pepper	*Freshly ground pepper*

Cooking Time: About 30 minutes

Melt the butter in a saucepan and fry the onion and garlic until soft but not brown. Add the vinegar, water or stock, mustard, sugar, lemon slice, bay leaf and cayenne. Bring slowly to the boil and simmer for 15 minutes. Stir in the remaining ingredients with salt and pepper to taste. Simmer for a further 5 to 10 minutes.

Remove the lemon slice and bay leaf before serving with barbecued meats.

Makes scant 300 ml (½ pint)

Tangy tartare sauce; Mayonnaise; Sweet and sour sauce; Spicy horseradish sauce

Mayonnaise

Metric	*Imperial*
1 egg yolk	*1 egg yolk*
125–250 ml salad or olive oil	*$\frac{1}{4}$–$\frac{1}{2}$ pint salad or olive oil*
Large pinch of dry mustard	*Large pinch of dry mustard*
Large pinch of salt	*Large pinch of salt*
Freshly ground pepper	*Freshly ground pepper*
1 × 15 ml spoon wine vinegar or lemon juice	*1 tablespoon wine vinegar or lemon juice*

The egg yolk and oil should be at cool room temperature. Place the egg yolk in a bowl together with the dry seasonings. Use a small hand mixer or wooden spoon and beat in the oil drop by drop. Once the mixture forms an emulsion, add the remaining oil in a thin stream. When the mixture becomes thick add a little of the vinegar or lemon juice. When all the oil has been incorporated, add the remaining vinegar or lemon juice. Taste and adjust the seasoning. The finished consistency should be like double cream.

To make mayonnaise in a blender, use a whole egg and add the oil in a thin stream with the blender on low speed. Serve with salads accompanying barbecued meats.

Makes about 150–300 ml ($\frac{1}{4}$–$\frac{1}{2}$ pint)

Tangy tartare sauce

Metric	*Imperial*
150 ml mayonnaise	*$\frac{1}{4}$ pint mayonnaise*
1 × 2.5 ml spoon grated onion	*$\frac{1}{2}$ teaspoon grated onion*
1 × 15 ml spoon chopped capers	*1 tablespoon chopped capers*
1 × 5 ml spoon chopped fresh parsley	*1 teaspoon chopped fresh parsley*
Salt	*Salt*
Freshly ground pepper	*Freshly ground pepper*

Mix all the ingredients together and allow to stand for 1 hour. Serve as an accompaniment to fish.

Makes about 150 ml ($\frac{1}{4}$ pint)

Sweet and sour sauce

Metric	*Imperial*
1 × 400 g can tomatoes	*1 × 14 oz can tomatoes*
2 green peppers, cored, seeded and diced	*2 green peppers, cored, seeded and diced*
2 × 15 ml spoons cornflour	*2 tablespoons cornflour*
4 × 15 ml spoons vinegar	*4 tablespoons vinegar*
2 × 15 ml spoons sugar	*2 tablespoons sugar*
150 ml tomato juice	*$\frac{1}{4}$ pint tomato juice*
1 × 15 ml spoon soy sauce	*1 tablespoon soy sauce*
Salt	*Salt*
Freshly ground pepper	*Freshly ground pepper*

Cooking Time: 15 minutes

Put the tomatoes with the can juice in a saucepan and break them down with a wooden spoon. Stir in the green peppers. Bring to the boil and simmer for 5 minutes. Dissolve the cornflour in the vinegar and add to the tomato mixture with the remaining ingredients and salt and pepper to taste. Stir well and cook for 10 minutes.

This sauce is ideal for serving with pork.

Makes about 300 ml ($\frac{1}{2}$ pint)

Variation:

Dice 2 slices of canned pineapple and cook for 10 minutes with the other ingredients.

Spicy horseradish sauce

Metric	*Imperial*
150 ml double cream	*$\frac{1}{4}$ pint double cream*
1 × 15 ml spoon lemon juice	*1 tablespoon lemon juice*
2 × 5 ml spoons peeled and grated horseradish	*2 teaspoons peeled and grated horseradish*
2 × 5 ml spoons Worcestershire sauce	*2 teaspoons Worcestershire sauce*
2 spring onions, finely chopped	*2 spring onions, finely chopped*

Whip the cream lightly but do not make it thick. Stir in the lemon juice, horseradish, Worcestershire sauce and spring onions. Allow to stand for about 4 hours in the refrigerator before serving.

Serve with hamburgers, barbecued steaks or skewered beef.

Makes about 150 ml ($\frac{1}{4}$ pint)

Pineapple and cider sauce; Mushroom sauce; French dressing; Provençale sauce; Seafood sauce

Provençale sauce

Metric	*Imperial*
2 × 15 ml spoons oil	*2 tablespoons oil*
1 large onion, peeled and finely chopped	*1 large onion, peeled and finely chopped*
1 garlic clove, crushed	*1 garlic clove, crushed*
1 aubergine, finely diced	*1 aubergine, finely diced*
1 green pepper, cored, seeded and finely diced	*1 green pepper, cored, seeded and finely diced*
50 g mushrooms, finely diced	*2 oz mushrooms, finely diced*
2 × 400 g cans tomatoes	*2 × 14 oz cans tomatoes*
150 ml stock	*¼ pint stock*
1 × 2.5 ml spoon dried oregano or thyme	*½ teaspoon dried oregano or thyme*
Salt	*Salt*
Freshly ground pepper	*Freshly ground pepper*

Cooking Time: 34 to 40 minutes

Heat the oil in a saucepan and fry the onion and garlic until soft but not brown. Add the aubergine, green pepper and mushrooms and cook for 5 minutes, stirring occasionally. Stir in the tomatoes with the can juice and break down with a wooden spoon. Add the stock, oregano or thyme and salt and pepper to taste. Bring to the boil and simmer for 30 minutes or until the vegetables are tender. Taste and adjust the seasoning.
Serve with fish or meat.
Makes about 300 ml (½ pint)

Pineapple and cider sauce

Metric	*Imperial*
1 × 15 ml spoon cornflour	*1 tablespoon cornflour*
300 ml dry cider	*½ pint dry cider*
100 g fresh or canned pineapple, chopped	*4 oz fresh or canned pineapple, chopped*
25 g seedless raisins	*1 oz seedless raisins*

Cooking Time: 5 minutes

Dissolve the cornflour in a little of the cider. Heat the remaining cider in a saucepan, then stir into the dissolved cornflour. Return to the saucepan and bring to the boil, stirring. Add the pineapple and raisins and heat through. Serve with gammon steaks or pork chops.

Makes about 300 ml (½ pint)

Mushroom sauce

Metric	*Imperial*
25 g butter	*1 oz butter*
1 onion, peeled and chopped	*1 onion, peeled and chopped*
175 g mushrooms, sliced	*6 oz mushrooms, sliced*
1 × 15 ml spoon plain flour	*1 tablespoon plain flour*
300 ml beef stock	*½ pint beef stock*
Few drops of Worcestershire sauce	*Few drops of Worcestershire sauce*
1 × 2.5 ml spoon soy sauce	*½ teaspoon soy sauce*
Salt	*Salt*
Freshly ground pepper	*Freshly ground pepper*

Cooking Time: About 10 minutes

Melt the butter in a saucepan and fry the onion until soft but not brown. Add the mushrooms and cook for about 2 minutes. Stir in the flour and cook for 1 minute. Remove from the heat and gradually stir in the stock. Return to the heat and bring to the boil. Stir in the Worcestershire sauce, soy sauce and salt and pepper to taste. Simmer gently for 3 to 4 minutes. Taste and adjust the seasoning.

Serve with beef skewers or hamburgers.

Makes about 300 ml (½ pint)

French dressing

Metric	*Imperial*
1 × 15 ml spoon wine vinegar	*1 tablespoon wine vinegar*
3 × 15 ml spoons salad or olive oil	*3 tablespoons salad or olive oil*
Pinch of salt	*Pinch of salt*
Pinch of pepper	*Pinch of pepper*
Pinch of dry mustard	*Pinch of dry mustard*
1 × 15 ml spoon chopped fresh herbs (optional)	*1 tablespoon chopped fresh herbs (optional)*

Put all the ingredients in a screw-topped jar and shake well to mix thoroughly. Serve with salads, but do not dress green salads until just before serving as lettuce becomes limp in French dressing after a short time.

Makes about 4 × 15 ml spoons (4 tablespoons)

Seafood sauce

Metric	*Imperial*
150 ml mayonnaise	*¼ pint mayonnaise*
1 × 15 ml spoon tomato purée	*1 tablespoon tomato purée*
1 × 5 ml spoon grated lemon rind	*1 teaspoon grated lemon rind*
2 × 15 ml spoons lemon juice	*2 tablespoons lemon juice*
1 × 5 ml spoon Worcestershire sauce	*1 teaspoon Worcestershire sauce*
Few drops of Tabasco	*Few drops of Tabasco*
1 × 5 ml spoon finely grated onion or spring onion	*1 teaspoon finely grated onion or spring onion*
1 × 15 ml spoon chopped fresh parsley	*1 tablespoon chopped fresh parsley*
Salt	*Salt*
Freshly ground pepper	*Freshly ground pepper*

Mix together all the ingredients with salt and pepper to taste. To make a really special sauce to serve with fish, carefully fold in 2–3 × 15 ml spoons (2–3 tablespoons) lightly whipped cream.

Makes a generous 150 ml (¼ pint)

Pepper relish

Metric	Imperial
1 green pepper, cored, seeded and diced	1 green pepper, cored, seeded and diced
1 red pepper, cored, seeded and diced	1 red pepper, cored, seeded and diced
1 small onion, peeled and finely chopped	1 small onion, peeled and finely chopped
2 × 15 ml spoons sugar	2 tablespoons sugar
4 × 15 ml spoons sherry or cider vinegar	4 tablespoons sherry or cider vinegar
Salt	Salt
Freshly ground pepper	Freshly ground pepper

Cooking Time: 20 minutes

Put the green and red peppers and onion in a saucepan of boiling salted water. Return to the boil, then remove from the heat, cover and leave for 20 minutes. Drain the vegetables well and return to the saucepan. Stir in the sugar, sherry or vinegar and salt and pepper to taste. Return to the heat and simmer for 15 minutes. Taste and adjust seasoning. Serve with barbecued meat and poultry.

Corn relish

Metric	Imperial
4 tomatoes, skinned, seeded and diced	4 tomatoes, skinned, seeded and diced
1 onion, peeled and diced	1 onion, peeled and diced
½ green pepper, cored, seeded and diced	½ green pepper, cored, seeded and diced
50 g frozen sweetcorn, blanched and drained	2 oz frozen sweetcorn, blanched and drained
1 celery stalk, diced	1 celery stalk, diced
2–3 dried red chilli peppers, chopped	2–3 dried red chilli peppers, chopped
2 × 15 ml spoons brown sugar	2 tablespoons brown sugar
6 × 15 ml spoons vinegar	6 tablespoons vinegar
1 × 2.5 ml spoon mustard seed	½ teaspoon mustard seed
1 × 2.5 ml spoon celery seed or celery salt	½ teaspoon celery seed or celery salt

Mix together the tomatoes, onion, green pepper, corn, celery and chilli peppers in a mixing bowl. Combine the remaining ingredients and pour over the vegetables.
Leave to stand for 24 hours before serving with barbecued poultry and skewered food.

Maître d'hôtel butter

Metric	Imperial
75 g butter, softened	3 oz butter, softened
Juice of ½ lemon	Juice of ½ lemon
1 × 15 ml spoon chopped fresh parsley	1 tablespoon chopped fresh parsley
Salt	Salt
Freshly ground pepper	Freshly ground pepper

Mix together all the ingredients with salt and pepper to taste. With cool, wet hands, shape into a roll about 3 cm (1½ inches) in diameter. Wrap in foil and chill well.
Serve with plain barbecued meats.

Variation:
To make Tarragon butter, substitute chopped fresh tarragon for the parsley.

Corn relish; Pepper relish; Garlic butter; Maître d'hôtel butter; Tarragon butter; Mustard butter; Bercy butter; Onion butter

Bercy butter

Metric	*Imperial*
150 ml white wine	*¼ pint white wine*
2 shallots, peeled and chopped	*2 shallots, peeled and chopped*
75 g butter, softened	*3 oz butter, softened*
Salt	*Salt*
Freshly ground pepper	*Freshly ground pepper*
1 × 5 ml spoon lemon juice	*1 teaspoon lemon juice*

Put the white wine and shallots in a saucepan and bring to the boil. Boil until the liquid has reduced almost to nothing. Allow to cool a little, then add the softened butter and stir until smooth. Add salt and pepper to taste and the lemon juice. With cool, wet hands, shape into a roll about 3 cm (1½ inches) in diameter. Wrap in foil and chill well.
This butter is delicious with plain barbecued chops or steaks.

Mustard butter

Metric	*Imperial*
50 g butter, softened	*2 oz butter, softened*
1 × 5 ml spoon dry mustard or 2 × 5 ml spoons prepared French mustard	*1 teaspoon dry mustard or 2 teaspoons prepared French mustard*
Salt	*Salt*
Freshly ground pepper	*Freshly ground pepper*

Mix together all the ingredients with salt and pepper to taste. With cool, wet hands, shape into a roll about 3 cm (1½ inches) in diameter. Wrap in foil and chill well.
Serve with sausages, hamburgers, steaks or chops.

Garlic butter

Metric	*Imperial*
50 g butter	*2 oz butter*
1–2 garlic cloves	*1–2 garlic cloves*
1 × 15 ml spoon finely chopped fresh parsley (optional)	*1 tablespoon finely chopped fresh parsley (optional)*

Cream the butter until soft. Press the garlic through a sieve or a garlic press. Beat the garlic and parsley into the butter until well mixed. Using cool, wet hands, shape into a roll about 3 cm (1½ inches) in diameter. Wrap in foil and chill well. Serve on beefburgers, chops and steaks.

To make garlic bread
Cut a French loaf into thick slices without cutting through the bottom 1 cm (½ inch). Spread garlic butter on both sides of each slice, press together and wrap in foil. Heat through on the side of the barbecue or in a preheated moderate oven (180°C, 350°F, Gas Mark 4) for about 15 minutes.

Onion butter

Metric	*Imperial*
50 g butter, softened	*2 oz butter, softened*
1 × 5 ml spoon Worcestershire sauce	*1 teaspoon Worcestershire sauce*
Large pinch of dry mustard	*Large pinch of dry mustard*
1 onion, peeled and grated	*1 onion, peeled and grated*
2 × 15 ml spoons chopped fresh parsley	*2 tablespoons chopped fresh parsley*
Freshly ground black pepper	*Freshly ground black pepper*

Mix together all the ingredients with pepper to taste. With cool, wet hands, form into a roll about 3 cm (1½ inches) in diameter. Wrap in foil and chill well.
Serve on beefburgers, chops or steaks.

FISH

To cook fish on the barbecue is simple provided the fish is fresh and firm. It should not be handled too much as the delicate flesh breaks up easily. A grill rack with a handle is ideal as the fish can be removed from the heat if it is too fierce, or turned without struggling with a fish slice over the heat. Fish should not be overcooked or it will become dry. Wash and gut quickly under cold running water but do not leave to soak. Be sure all frozen fish is completely thawed.

Small metal smoke boxes are fairly cheap to buy and ideal for smoke-cooking fish if you are on a fishing trip. A small methylated spirit burner burns wood chips, and in about 10 minutes your fish are smoke-cooked and ready to eat.

Large fish such as salmon or salmon trout, if you are lucky enough to have them, may be cooked on the spit whole. Salmon is an oily fish so it doesn't need to be basted, but it tastes even better brushed over with oil or Lemon Marinade (see page 17) towards the end of the cooking time, when the skin will be black and crisp.

Fish cakes are extra tasty when cooked on the barbecue, and small shellfish are excellent for skewer cooking. Fish on skewers take only a short time to cook and make delicious starters while the main course is cooking.

Barbecued trout

Metric	*Imperial*
50 g butter, melted	*2 oz butter, melted*
2 × 15 ml spoons lemon juice	*2 tablespoons lemon juice*
2 × 15 ml spoons chopped fresh parsley	*2 tablespoons chopped fresh parsley*
Salt	*Salt*
Freshly ground pepper	*Freshly ground pepper*
4 trout, cleaned and washed	*4 trout, cleaned and washed*

Cooking Time: About 15 to 20 minutes

Mix together the butter, lemon juice, parsley and salt and pepper to taste. Brush the trout inside and out with the butter mixture. Cook on the grid on the barbecue, turning several times and brushing with the lemon butter towards the end of the cooking time.

Barbecued trout

Barbecued salmon steaks

Metric	*Imperial*
4 salmon steaks	*4 salmon steaks*
4 × 15 ml spoons oil	*4 tablespoons oil*
1 × 5 ml spoon chopped fresh rosemary or 1 × 2.5 ml spoon dried rosemary	*1 teaspoon chopped fresh rosemary or ½ teaspoon dried rosemary*
Salt	*Salt*
Freshly ground pepper	*Freshly ground pepper*
Fresh rosemary sprigs (if available)	*Fresh rosemary sprigs (if available)*
4 lemon wedges, to serve	*4 lemon wedges, to serve*

Cooking Time: About 10 to 20 minutes, depending on thickness

Lay the salmon steaks in a shallow dish. Mix the oil, rosemary and salt and pepper to taste together and brush over both sides of the steaks. Pour the remainder of the oil mixture on top of the steaks and leave to marinate for at least 30 minutes.

Brush the barbecue grid with a little of the oil mixture. Place a few sprigs of fresh rosemary, if available, on the charcoal. The salmon should be cooked on a medium hot fire and turned and brushed with the oil marinade from time to time. Watch the fish carefully while it is cooking to avoid it breaking up. Serve with lemon wedges and Hollandaise Sauce.

Whole fish barbecue

Metric	*Imperial*
1 × 1.5–2 kg sea bass, bream or salmon trout, cleaned and washed	*1 × 3–4 lb sea bass, bream or salmon trout, cleaned and washed*
White Wine Barbecue Marinade (see page 15)	*White Wine Barbecue Marinade (see page 15)*
4 fresh fennel sprigs	*4 fresh fennel sprigs*
Lemon wedges, to serve	*Lemon wedges, to serve*

Cooking Time: About 45 to 60 minutes (15 minutes to each 500 g/1 lb)

Put the fish on a large double sheet of foil and fold up the sides. Pour over the marinade. Leave to marinate for 2 to 4 hours in the refrigerator. Put the fennel sprigs inside the fish and place the open foil parcel on the barbecue grid. Cook until the fish is tender, brushing with the marinade in the foil to keep the fish moist.

Serves with wedges of lemon.

Spanish barbecued sprats

Metric	*Imperial*
750 g sprats, cleaned and washed	*1½ lb sprats, cleaned and washed*
Lemon Marinade (see page 17)	*Lemon Marinade (see page 17)*
4 lemon wedges, to serve	*4 lemon wedges, to serve*

Cooking Time: About 10 minutes

Wash the sprats under cold running water and place in the lemon marinade. Leave to marinate for about 30 minutes. Thread the fish on long skewers and cook about 5 to 7 cm (2 to 3 inches) away from the fire. These little fish are crispy and delicious and make an ideal starter for a barbecue meal served with lemon wedges and Tangy Tartare Sauce.

Fish cakes

Metric	*Imperial*
350 g smoked haddock or whiting	*12 oz smoked haddock or whiting*
350 g potatoes, cooked and peeled	*12 oz potatoes, cooked and peeled*
Knob of butter	*Knob of butter*
2 × 15 ml spoons chopped fresh parsley	*2 tablespoons chopped fresh parsley*
Salt	*Salt*
Freshly ground black pepper	*Freshly ground black pepper*
Beaten egg for binding	*Beaten egg for binding*
Oil	*Oil*
Lemon wedges, to serve	*Lemon wedges, to serve*

Cooking Time: 10 minutes

Poach the fish, drain and flake. Mash the potatoes and add the knob of butter. Mix together the fish and potato, then stir in the parsley with salt and pepper to taste. Bind the mixture with beaten egg. Shape into an oblong on a floured board and cut into 10 portions. Shape each portion into a cake. Chill for 30 minutes.

Brush the fish cakes with oil and place on the barbecue grid. Cook until lightly browned on both sides. Serve with lemon wedges and Tomato Sauce.

Whole fish barbecue; Barbecued mackerel; Salmon steaks; Fish cakes; Spanish barbecued sprats

Barbecued mackerel

Metric	*Imperial*
25 g butter, melted	*1 oz butter, melted*
1 × 5 ml spoon dried fennel or 4 fresh fennel sprigs	*1 teaspoon dried fennel or 4 fresh fennel sprigs*
1 × 5 ml spoon finely diced onion	*1 teaspoon finely diced onion*
2 × 15 ml spoons lemon juice	*2 tablespoons lemon juice*
½ × 150 ml carton plain unsweetened yogurt	*½ × 5 fl oz carton plain unsweetened yogurt*
Salt	*Salt*
Freshly ground pepper	*Freshly ground pepper*
4 mackerel, cleaned and washed	*4 mackerel, cleaned and washed*
1 × 15 ml spoon oil	*1 tablespoon oil*

Cooking Time: About 20 to 30 minutes

Mix together the butter, fennel, onion, lemon juice, yogurt and salt and pepper to taste. Brush a little of the mixture inside the fish. Brush the outside of the fish with oil and place on a double sheet of foil on the barbecue grid. Turn and baste several times with oil while cooking, and brush inside with the yogurt mixture.

Gently heat the remaining yogurt mixture in a saucepan on the side of the barbecue and serve as a sauce with the fish. Alternatively, serve the fish with Spicy Horseradish Sauce.

BEEF

The special flavour of good-quality steak or beef cooked on the barbecue outdoors is hard to better. Being so expensive, beef must be carefully cooked, so ensure a good glowing medium hot fire to keep the meat well sealed but not burnt on the outside, and moist inside.

Prepare steaks by slitting the fat round the edge every 2.5 cm (1 inch) to avoid curling during cooking. Do not salt before cooking as this tends to draw out the moisture. Seal the steaks on both sides on a hot fire, then move the grid away from the fire to cook over a medium heat.

To spit-roast joints of beef read the information on spit-roasting in the introduction on pages 6–7. Always have a small drip tray to catch the juice from the meat, and ensure that the joint is correctly balanced to avoid strain on the motor turning it round. Jerky, uneven movements will not produce evenly browned food, and will eventually break the rôtisserie. Exact cooking times will depend on the heat of the fire. Unless your barbecue has a powerful motor it is better to roast boned joints; wing ribs and similar joints are difficult to balance on the average-sized model.

All beef should be thawed if necessary, and brought to room temperature before cooking.

Suitable cuts for the barbecue and approximate cooking times

Sirloin cut into steaks;	12–20 minutes
boned and rolled	20 minutes per pound
Wing ribs cut into steaks *Rump* cut into steaks or skewered	7–15 minutes depending whether to be served rare or well done
Fillet cut into steaks;	7–10 minutes
spit-roasted wrapped or barded with fat to baste it	15 minutes per pound
Topside (as this is so lean it is better marinated first; or use for skewered cooking)	25 minutes per pound
Chuck or flank, finely minced with 15% fat for hamburgers 2.5 cm (1 inch) thick	15–20 minutes

Barbecued sirloin

Metric	*Imperial*
1 × 1.5–2 kg boned and rolled sirloin	*1 × 3–4 lb boned and rolled sirloin*
Freshly ground pepper	*Freshly ground pepper*
2 × 15 ml spoons oil	*2 tablespoons oil*
1 × 5 ml spoon Worcestershire sauce	*1 teaspoon Worcestershire sauce*

Cooking Time: About 50 minutes to 1¼ hours

Insert the rôtisserie spit carefully into the sirloin. Season well with pepper and brush over with a mixture of oil and Worcestershire sauce. Cook over a good glowing fire, basting with the oil mixture from time to time. The flavour of barbecued beef is excellent, but a Red Wine Barbecue Marinade (see page 14) may be used to enhance it.
Serve with Barbecued Baked Potatoes and a mixed salad.
Serves 6 to 8

Barbecued baked potatoes

Metric	*Imperial*
4 even-sized potatoes, scrubbed and pricked	*4 even-sized potatoes, scrubbed and pricked*
1 avocado, halved and stoned	*1 avocado, halved and stoned*
125 g cream cheese	*4 oz cream cheese*
Salt	*Salt*
Freshly ground pepper	*Freshly ground pepper*

Cooking Time: About 45 minutes to 1 hour

Parboil the potatoes for 15 to 20 minutes or bake in a preheated moderate oven (180°C, 350°F, Gas Mark 4) for 30 minutes. Place on the barbecue grid and cook for a further 30 minutes or until soft.
Halve the potatoes and scoop out some of the flesh into a bowl. Scoop the avocado flesh from the skins and add to the potato with the cream cheese and salt and pepper to taste. Mix thoroughly together. Pile the filling back into the potato skins and return to the barbecue to heat through.

Barbecued sirloin; Barbecued baked potatoes

Variations for potato fillings

Cottage cheese and chives

Metric	*Imperial*
125 g cottage cheese	*4 oz cottage cheese*
1 × 15 ml spoon chopped fresh chives	*1 tablespoon chopped fresh chives*
Salt	*Salt*
Freshly ground pepper	*Freshly ground pepper*

Beat the cottage cheese very thoroughly and add the chives and salt and pepper to taste. If you prefer a smooth filling, mix the ingredients with a hand mixer or blender. Add to the potato flesh instead of the avocado and cream cheese.

Savoury cream cheese

Metric	*Imperial*
125 g cream cheese	*4 oz cream cheese*
1 small onion, peeled and finely chopped	*1 small onion, peeled and finely chopped*
1 × 15 ml spoon chopped fresh parsley	*1 tablespoon chopped fresh parsley*
Salt	*Salt*
Freshly ground pepper	*Freshly ground pepper*

Cream all the ingredients together thoroughly with salt and pepper to taste. Add to the potato flesh in place of the avocado and cream cheese.

Cheeseburgers

Metric	*Imperial*
500 g lean minced beef	*1 lb lean minced beef*
50 g cheese, grated	*2 oz cheese, grated*
1 onion, peeled and grated	*1 onion, peeled and grated*
4 × 15 ml spoons crushed cornflakes	*4 tablespoons crushed cornflakes*
Few drops of Worcestershire sauce	*Few drops of Worcestershire sauce*
Salt	*Salt*
Freshly ground pepper	*Freshly ground pepper*

Cooking Time: About 10 minutes

Put all the ingredients in a bowl with salt and pepper to taste and mix well together. Form the mixture into 8 cakes using a 5 cm (2 inch) scone cutter. Place in the refrigerator and chill well. Brush the barbecue grid with oil and cook for 5 minutes on each side.

If liked, the cheeseburgers can be topped with a slice of cheese and served in heated soft rolls.

Beachburgers

Metric	*Imperial*
500 g lean minced beef	*1 lb lean minced beef*
1 green pepper, cored, seeded and finely chopped	*1 green pepper, cored, seeded and finely chopped*
1 garlic clove, minced	*1 garlic clove, minced*
2 spring onions, finely chopped	*2 spring onions, finely chopped*
2 × 15 ml spoons chopped fresh parsley	*2 tablespoons chopped fresh parsley*
Large pinch of paprika	*Large pinch of paprika*
Salt	*Salt*
Freshly ground pepper	*Freshly ground pepper*

Cooking Time: About 10 minutes

Put all the ingredients in a bowl with salt and pepper to taste and mix well together. Form into six cakes using a 5 cm (2 inch) scone cutter. Chill well before cooking on an oiled barbecue grid for about 5 minutes on each side. Serve with Creole Sauce.

Irish hamburgers

Metric	*Imperial*
500 g lean minced beef	*1 lb lean minced beef*
2 medium potatoes, peeled and grated	*2 medium potatoes, peeled and grated*
1 medium onion, peeled and finely chopped	*1 medium onion, peeled and finely chopped*
2 × 15 ml spoons chopped fresh parsley	*2 tablespoons chopped fresh parsley*
Few drops of Worcestershire sauce	*Few drops of Worcestershire sauce*
Salt	*Salt*
Freshly ground pepper	*Freshly ground pepper*

Cooking Time: About 10 minutes

Put all the ingredients with salt and pepper to taste in a bowl and mix well together. Form into eight cakes using a 5 cm (2 inch) scone cutter. Chill well before cooking on an oiled barbecue grid for about 5 minutes on each side. Serve topped with sliced tomato.

Cheeseburgers; Beachburgers; Irish hamburgers; Tomato hamburgers

Tomato hamburgers

Metric	*Imperial*
600 g lean minced beef	*1¼ lb lean minced beef*
50 g fresh breadcrumbs	*2 oz fresh breadcrumbs*
150 ml Tomato Sauce (see page 19)	*¼ pint Tomato Sauce (see page 19)*
1 large onion, peeled and finely chopped	*1 large onion, peeled and finely chopped*
1 2.5 ml spoon dried chervil or 1 × 15 ml spoon chopped fresh parsley	*½ teaspoon dried chervil or 1 tablespoon chopped fresh parsley*
1 × 5 ml spoon Tabasco sauce	*1 teaspoon Tabasco sauce*
Salt	*Salt*
Freshly ground pepper	*Freshly ground pepper*

Cooking Time: About 10 minutes

Put all the ingredients in a bowl with salt and pepper to taste and mix well together. Form into 10 cakes using a 5 cm (2 inch) scone cutter. Chill well, then cook on an oiled barbecue grid for about 5 minutes on each side.

LAMB

Use only tender young lamb for barbecueing. It should be thawed if necessary and brought to room temperature before being cooked. Frozen lamb may be thawed in a marinade for extra flavour.

Leg of lamb can be cut into cubes and used for skewer cooking outdoors; these kebabs make a change from roast lamb and are less trouble to cook on a warm day.

Suitable cuts for the barbecue and approximate cooking times

Best end cut into chops; or boned, rolled and cut into slices or noisettes	10–15 minutes
Breast (must be marinated first), cut into riblets	30–60 minutes
Chump chops	10–15 minutes
Gigot chops	20–25 minutes
Leg spit-roasted with or without bone;	25 minutes per pound
cut into steaks or diced and cooked on skewers	8–15 minutes
Loin chops	15–20 minutes
Shoulder, boned and rolled	25 minutes per pound
Kidney, skewered	10 minutes
Liver, skewered	10–15 minutes
Lamburgers	15 minutes

Barbecued boned leg of lamb

Metric	*Imperial*
1 × 1.5 kg leg of lamb, boned	*1 × 3 lb leg of lamb, boned*
4 × 15 ml spoons oil	*4 tablespoons oil*
2 × 15 ml spoons wine vinegar	*2 tablespoons wine vinegar*
1 × 5 ml spoon salt	*1 teaspoon salt*
Large pinch of pepper	*Large pinch of pepper*
Large pinch of garlic powder or 1 garlic clove, crushed	*Large pinch of garlic powder or 1 garlic clove, crushed*
Creole Sauce (see page 18)	*Creole Sauce (see page 18)*

Cooking Time: About 1½ hours (or longer for well-cooked lamb)

Flatten the lamb with a rolling pin or a cutlet bat. Put in a shallow dish. Mix together the oil, vinegar, salt, pepper and garlic and pour over the lamb. Leave to marinate in the refrigerator for at least 2 hours.
Place the meat on the barbecue grid and cook over a medium heat, turning every 10 to 15 minutes. Baste with hot Creole Sauce towards the end of the cooking.

Stuffed shoulder of lamb

Metric	*Imperial*
1 × 2 kg shoulder of lamb, boned	*1 × 4 lb shoulder of lamb, boned*
50 g fresh breadcrumbs	*2 oz fresh breadcrumbs*
1 × 2.5 ml spoon dried rosemary or 1 × 5 ml spoon chopped fresh rosemary	*½ teaspoon dried rosemary or 1 teaspoon chopped fresh rosemary*
4 canned peach halves, chopped	*4 canned peach halves, chopped*
½ egg, beaten	*½ egg, beaten*
Salt	*Salt*
Freshly ground pepper	*Freshly ground pepper*
Oil	*Oil*

Cooking Time: About 1 hour (or longer for well-cooked lamb)

Open out the boned shoulder of lamb and trim off excess fat. Mix together the breadcrumbs, rosemary, peaches and egg with salt and pepper to taste. Spread on the lamb and roll up. Secure tightly with string. Brush with oil and sprinkle with pepper. Insert the rôtisserie spit into the meat and cook, basting with oil, or oil and rosemary, from time to time.

Stuffed shoulder of lamb; Barbecued boned leg of lamb

Barbecued French leg of lamb

Metric	*Imperial*
2 × 15 ml spoons oil	*2 tablespoons oil*
2 × 15 ml spoons white wine	*2 tablespoons white wine*
Salt	*Salt*
Freshly ground pepper	*Freshly ground pepper*
1 × 1.5–2 kg leg of lamb	*1 × 3–4 lb leg of lamb*
2 garlic cloves, cut into slivers	*2 garlic cloves, cut into slivers*
10 fresh rosemary sprigs	*10 fresh rosemary sprigs*

Cooking Time: About 1½ to 2 hours (or slightly longer for well-cooked lamb)

Mix together the oil, wine and salt and pepper to taste and brush a little over the leg of lamb. Make slits in the skin of the lamb and insert the garlic slivers and rosemary sprigs. Put the lamb in a polythene bag with the remaining oil and wine mixture. Leave to marinate in the refrigerator for 2 to 4 hours, turning from time to time to ensure the marinade soaks into all parts of the meat.
Remove from the bag and insert the rôtisserie spit carefully into the lamb. Be sure to balance the leg carefully so that the rôtisserie can work without the strain of the heavy end upsetting the balance. You will need a fairly large fire to give enough heat to cook a leg of lamb. Make sure it is hot and glowing before starting the cooking. Brush the leg with the marinade from time to time and put a few sprigs of rosemary on the fire for extra flavour. The flavour of this lamb is excellent, especially if served slightly pink.
Serves 4 to 6

Spicy barbecued lamb

Metric	*Imperial*
1 × 2 kg breast of lamb	*1 × 4 lb breast of lamb*
Lemon wedges, to garnish	*Lemon wedges, to garnish*
Cider Marinade:	Cider Marinade:
150 ml dry cider	*¼ pint dry cider*
2 × 15 ml spoons Worcestershire sauce	*2 tablespoons Worcestershire sauce*
1 × 15 ml spoon brown sugar	*1 tablespoon brown sugar*
2 × 15 ml spoons oil	*2 tablespoons oil*
2 × 15 ml spoons wine or cider vinegar	*2 tablespoons wine or cider vinegar*
1 medium onion, peeled and finely chopped	*1 medium onion, peeled and finely chopped*
1 × 2.5 ml spoon dried rosemary	*½ teaspoon dried rosemary*
Salt	*Salt*
Freshly ground pepper	*Freshly ground pepper*

Cooking Time: About 45 to 60 minutes

Remove the excess fat from the lamb and cut the meat into strips between the bones with a sharp knife. Place all the marinade ingredients with salt and pepper to taste in a pan and bring to the boil. Simmer gently for 3 to 4 minutes, then leave to cool. Put the lamb in a bowl, pour over the marinade and leave to marinate in the refrigerator for at least 3 hours, turning occasionally.
Place the lamb on the barbecue grid and cook until crispy, basting occasionally with the marinade. Serve hot, piled on a large platter and garnished with lemon wedges. Heat the remaining marinade and serve separately.

Barbecued gigot chops

Metric	*Imperial*
4 gigot (leg) lamb chops	*4 gigot (leg) lamb chops*
Oil	*Oil*
Freshly ground pepper	*Freshly ground pepper*
Salt	*Salt*
Chopped fresh parsley, to garnish	*Chopped fresh parsley, to garnish*

Cooking Time: About 25 minutes

If necessary, trim excess fat from the chops. Brush with oil and season with pepper. Place the chops on the barbecue grid and cook, turning occasionally. Sprinkle with a little salt and arrange on a warmed serving plate garnished with parsley. Sprinkle a little chopped parsley on top of each chop.
Serve with Smoky Barbecue Sauce.

Spicy barbecued lamb; Barbecued French leg of lamb; Barbecued gigot chops; Grilled lamb steaks

Grilled lamb steaks

Metric	*Imperial*
1 × 1.5 kg leg of lamb, boned	*1 × 3 lb leg of lamb, boned*
Salt	*Salt*
Freshly ground pepper	*Freshly ground pepper*
50 g Maître d'Hôtel Butter (see page 24), softened	*2 oz Maître d'Hôtel Butter (see page 24), softened*

Cooking Time: About 15 to 20 minutes

Cut the lamb into steaks about 2.5 cm (1 inch) thick. Trim off excess fat and rub both sides with salt and pepper. Brush with the softened butter. Barbecue over a good red heat, turning occasionally. Like beef, lamb steaks are best left slightly pink in the centre.
Serve with barbecued tomatoes and watercress salad.

Barbecued breast of lamb

Metric	*Imperial*
2 × 2 kg breasts of lamb	*2 × 4 lb breasts of lamb*
1 litre boiling water	*1¾ pints boiling water*
2 × 15 ml spoons vinegar	*2 tablespoons vinegar*
Sauce:	Sauce:
2 × 15 ml spoons soy sauce	*2 tablespoons soy sauce*
2 × 15 ml spoons clear honey	*2 tablespoons clear honey*
2 × 15 ml spoons plum jam	*2 tablespoons plum jam*
1 × 15 ml spoon white wine vinegar	*1 tablespoon white wine vinegar*
1 × 5 ml spoon Worcestershire sauce	*1 teaspoon Worcestershire sauce*
1 × 5 ml spoon dry mustard	*1 teaspoon dry mustard*
1 × 5 ml spoon tomato ketchup	*1 teaspoon tomato ketchup*
Squeeze of lemon juice	*Squeeze of lemon juice*

Cooking Time: About 30 to 40 minutes

Remove the excess fat from the lamb and cut the meat into strips between the bones with a sharp knife. Put into a saucepan and pour over the boiling water and vinegar. Simmer for 15 minutes. Mix all the sauce ingredients together in another saucepan and heat slowly. Drain the lamb and brush with the sauce. Put on the barbecue grid and cook, turning occasionally and basting with the sauce. Serve piled on a large platter with any remaining sauce.
Serves 6

Devilled lamb chops

Metric	*Imperial*
4 lamb chump chops	*4 lamb chump chops*
Salt	*Salt*
Freshly ground pepper	*Freshly ground pepper*
4 × 5 ml spoons prepared French mustard	*4 teaspoons prepared French mustard*
4 × 15 ml spoons brown sugar	*4 tablespoons brown sugar*

Cooking Time: About 10 minutes (or longer for well-cooked lamb)

Trim the chops, season with salt and pepper and spread with half the mustard and half the sugar. Place on the barbecue grid and cook gently for 5 minutes. Turn over and spread with the remaining mustard and sugar. Cook for a further 5 minutes.

Minted lamb noisettes

Metric	*Imperial*
1 best end neck of lamb, boned and rolled	*1 best end neck of lamb, boned and rolled*
1 × 15 ml spoon white wine vinegar	*1 tablespoon white wine vinegar*
1 large bunch of fresh mint, finely chopped	*1 large bunch of fresh mint, finely chopped*
½ × 150 ml carton plain unsweetened yogurt	*½ × 5 fl oz carton plain unsweetened yogurt*
Salt	*Salt*
Freshly ground pepper	*Freshly ground pepper*

Cooking Time: About 10 minutes (or longer for well-cooked lamb)

Cut the lamb into 8 slices (noisettes) and arrange in one layer in a shallow dish. Mix together the vinegar, mint, yogurt and salt and pepper to taste. Pour over the lamb and turn the noisettes to coat with the yogurt mixture. Leave to marinate for 2 to 4 hours in the refrigerator.
Brush the barbecue grid with oil and arrange the noisettes on the grid. Cook for about 5 minutes on each side or until pink and juicy.
Serve with Pilaff and barbecued tomatoes.
The yogurt mixture may be heated gently and served separately as a sauce.

Minted lamb noisettes; Barbecued breast of lamb; Devilled lamb chops

Lamb patties

Metric	*Imperial*
750 g lean lamb, finely minced	*$1\frac{1}{2}$ lb lean lamb, finely minced*
1.5 × 5 ml spoons salt	*$1\frac{1}{2}$ teaspoons salt*
Freshly ground pepper	*Freshly ground pepper*
1 × 15 ml spoon chopped fresh mint or 1 × 5 ml spoon dried mint	*1 tablespoon chopped fresh mint or 1 teaspoon dried mint*
2 × 15 ml spoons milk	*2 tablespoons milk*
8 streaky bacon rashers, rinds removed	*8 streaky bacon rashers, rinds removed*

Cooking Time: 18 to 20 minutes

Mix the lamb with the salt, pepper, mint and milk. Divide the mixture into 8 square patties. Allow to chill until firm. Wrap the bacon around the patties and fix firmly with a small skewer. Barbecue for 8 to 9 minutes on each side.

Lamburgers

Metric	*Imperial*
600 g lamb, finely minced	*$1\frac{1}{4}$ lb lamb, finely minced*
2 × 15 ml spoons oil	*2 tablespoons oil*
1 garlic clove, crushed	*1 garlic clove, crushed*
2 × 15 ml spoons chopped fresh parsley	*2 tablespoons chopped fresh parsley*
Large pinch of dried rosemary	*Large pinch of dried rosemary*
Salt	*Salt*
Freshly ground pepper	*Freshly ground pepper*

Cooking Time: About 15 minutes

Mix the lamb with 1 × 15 ml spoon (1 tablespoon) of the oil, the garlic, herbs and salt and pepper to taste. Form the mixture into 8 cakes. Chill until firm, then brush with the remaining oil. Cook on the barbecue grid until golden brown, turning from time to time.
Serve with Courgette and Tomato Skewers.

Cheesy frankfurters

Metric	*Imperial*
8 frankfurter sausages	*8 frankfurter sausages*
8 × 5 cm narrow strips of processed cheese slices	*8 × 2 inch narrow strips of processed cheese slices*
8 bacon rashers, rinds removed	*8 bacon rashers, rinds removed*
8 long finger rolls	*8 long finger rolls*

Cooking Time: About 7 minutes

Split the frankfurters down the centre and insert a strip of cheese. Wrap each frankfurter in bacon and barbecue until the bacon is cooked. Meanwhile, heat the rolls round the edge of the fire.
This is an excellent meal for children who are too impatient to wait for barbecued dinners.

Porkburgers; Cheesy frankfurters; Lamburgers; Lamb patties

Porkburgers

Metric	*Imperial*
500 g pork sausagemeat or minced pork	*1 lb pork sausagemeat or minced pork*
2 bacon rashers, rinds removed, minced or finely chopped	*2 bacon rashers, rinds removed, minced or finely chopped*
2 × 5 ml spoons Worcestershire sauce	*2 teaspoons Worcestershire sauce*
1 small onion, peeled and grated	*1 small onion, peeled and grated*
2 × 15 ml spoons fresh white breadcrumbs	*2 tablespoons fresh white breadcrumbs*
Salt	*Salt*
Freshly ground pepper	*Freshly ground pepper*
2 × 5 ml spoons oil	*2 teaspoons oil*

Cooking Time: About 15 minutes

Mix the sausagemeat or minced pork with the bacon, Worcestershire sauce, onion, breadcrumbs, and salt and pepper to taste. Shape into 6 cakes using a 6.5 cm ($2\frac{1}{2}$ inch) pastry cutter. Chill until firm. Brush with oil and cook over a hot barbecue, turning occasionally.
Serve topped with sliced tomatoes and placed in heated rolls.
Serves 6

PORK

As pork should be cooked thoroughly it is unwise to roast joints over the barbecue unless it is very large and you are prepared to build the fire up to ensure that the joint is cooked right through.
If you are cooking large joints use a meat thermometer. Legs of pork are, in any case, too heavy for the average rôtisserie and it is easier to barbecue chops and leg cut into pieces and placed on skewers. Barbecued pork chops have an excellent flavour, but do make sure they are well cooked inside.

Pork fillets or tenderloins, cut into cubes, make delicious skewered dishes and can be marinated for extra tenderness and flavour.

Pork goes bad quickly in hot weather, so it should be kept refrigerated and only brought to room temperature when it is needed for the barbecue. Frozen pork must be thawed first.

Suitable cuts for the barbecue and approximate cooking times

Cut	Time
Chump loin chops and *spare rib chops* 2.5 cm (1 inch) thick	20–25 minutes
Leg and *fillet (tenderloin)* 2.5 cm (1 inch) thick	15–20 minutes
Chinese spare ribs–long bones from belly of pork; less time if boiled first	45 minutes–1 hour
Sausages	10–15 minutes
Chipolatas, skewered to stop them falling through the grid	7–10 minutes

Barbecued pork spare ribs

Metric	*Imperial*
1.75–2 kg Chinese spare ribs	*4 lb Chinese spare ribs*
Double quantity Oriental Marinade (see page 13)	*Double quantity Oriental Marinade (see page 13)*

Cooking Time: About 1 to $1\frac{1}{2}$ hours

Place the spare ribs in a polythene bag with the Oriental Marinade and leave in the refrigerator to marinate for 4 to 8 hours. Turn the ribs frequently to ensure even coverage. You will need a fairly large hot fire as spare ribs take quite a time to cook. Either arrange on a spit or on a grid and turn frequently. The ribs will have to be carefully tended as a great deal of fat comes out during cooking, and will flame. Baste with the marinade towards the end of cooking time and cook until crisp and brown on the outside and juicy inside.
Serve with plenty of paper napkins and a selection of sauces like Smoky Barbecue, Sweet and Sour or Corn Relish.

Variation:
To remove excess fat, the spare ribs may be first cooked in boiling water to cover for 30 minutes. Drain well, then brush with oil or marinade and barbecue for about 15 to 25 minutes.

Barbecued fillet

Metric	*Imperial*
500 g pork fillet (tenderloin), cubed	*$1\frac{1}{4}$ lb pork fillet (tenderloin), cubed*
1 green pepper, cored, seeded and cut into 2.5 cm squares	*1 green pepper, cored, seeded and cut into 1 inch squares*
1 × 200 g can pineapple chunks, drained	*1 × 7 oz can pineapple chunks, drained*
Oriental Marinade (see page 13)	*Oriental Marinade (see page 13)*
4 tomatoes	*4 tomatoes*

Cooking Time: About 20 minutes

Put the pork, green pepper and pineapple in a shallow dish. Pour over the marinade and turn to coat. Leave to marinate in the refrigerator for 2 hours.
Thread the pork, green pepper and pineapple alternately onto skewers, leaving space for a whole tomato at the end. Cook over a medium hot fire, turning occasionally and brushing with the marinade from time to time. Place the tomatoes on the ends of the skewers for the last 5 minutes. Serve with Pilaff, a green salad and Sweet and Sour Sauce.

Barbecued fillet; Barbecued pork chops; Barbecued pork spare ribs

Barbecued pork chops

Metric	*Imperial*
Onion Butter (see page 25)	*Onion Butter (see page 25)*
4 thick pork loin chops with kidney	*4 thick pork loin chops with kidney*
Salt	*Salt*
Freshly ground pepper	*Freshly ground pepper*

Cooking Time: About 20 minutes

Cut the onion butter into eight portions. Make a slit into the meat on the fat-covered side of each chop to make a pocket and stuff with a portion of the onion butter. Squeeze the slit together and remove any excess butter from the outside of the chop. Rub the chops with salt and pepper. Place on an oiled barbecue grid and cook over a good glowing heat. Serve with a pat of Onion Butter on each chop. Excellent with Barbecued Baked Potatoes and Corn on the Cob.

POULTRY

Chicken, turkey and duck are all well suited to barbecue cooking. Portions of any of them can be marinated for extra flavour, and it is an excellent idea to thaw frozen poultry in a marinade.

To cook a whole chicken on a spit, truss it securely, keeping the wings and legs close to the body and the neck skin skewered down. Drive the spit in from a point just in front of the parson's nose and bring it out around the top of the wishbone.

Place the spit on the motor and roast over a medium hot fire. The exact cooking time will depend on the fire and the air temperature, but allow about 2 hours for a 2 kg (4½ lb) bird. A barbecue with a hood will reflect heat and shorten the cooking time.

Baste a chicken with butter or oil throughout the cooking period, but only towards the end with a marinade or sauce.

A duck can also be spit roasted, and is excellent basted with Honey Basting Sauce (see page 15).

Chicken on a spit

Metric	*Imperial*
1 × 1.5 kg chicken	*1 × 3½ lb chicken*
Juice of ½ lemon	*Juice of ½ lemon*
Salt	*Salt*
Freshly ground pepper	*Freshly ground pepper*
1 bunch of mixed fresh herbs	*1 bunch of mixed fresh herbs*
Smoky Barbecue Sauce (see page 19)	*Smoky Barbecue Sauce (see page 19)*

Cooking Time: About 1 to 1¼ hours

Wipe the chicken and rub inside with lemon juice. Season well inside and out with salt and pepper. Stuff a mixed bunch of fresh herbs into the cavity. Insert the rôtisserie spit carefully into the chicken, distributing the weight evenly. Brush with Smoky Barbecue Sauce and roast over hot coals. Baste with the sauce several times during cooking for a crisp brown chicken.
Serve with Barbecued Corn on the Cob and Baked Potatoes. Heat the remaining Smoky Barbecue Sauce to serve with the chicken.

Variation:
Place chopped fresh tarragon mixed with butter in the cavity. Baste with a mixture of chopped fresh tarragon and melted butter instead of Smoky Barbecue Sauce.

Barbecued corn on the cob

Metric	*Imperial*
4 corn on the cobs	*4 corn on the cobs*
125 g butter	*4 oz butter*
1 × 15 ml spoon finely chopped fresh parsley	*1 tablespoon finely chopped fresh parsley*
Salt	*Salt*
Freshly ground pepper	*Freshly ground pepper*

Cooking Time: About 30 to 40 minutes

Fold back the husks from the corn and remove the silky hairs. Cut out the cob but retain the husk. Blanch the corn in boiling salted water for 7 minutes. Drain and replace in the husks. Place on the barbecue to cook with the meat. Really fresh corn can be cooked without blanching, but often the corn we buy is a little tough.
Mix the butter, parsley and salt and pepper to taste together to serve with the hot corn.

Variation:
Remove the husks and place the corn in foil parcels with the parsley butter. Seal the parcel tightly enough to prevent the butter from seeping out as this will cause flames on the barbecue. Cook for 20 to 25 minutes or until corn is tender.

Chicken on a spit; Barbecued corn on the cob

Chicken drumstick barbecue

Metric	*Imperial*
8 chicken drumsticks	*8 chicken drumsticks*
Red Wine Barbecue Marinade (see page 15)	*Red Wine Barbecue Marinade (see page 15)*
150 ml chicken stock	*$\frac{1}{4}$ pint chicken stock*
1 × 15 ml spoon tomato purée	*1 tablespoon tomato purée*
15 g butter	*$\frac{1}{2}$ oz butter*
2 × 5 ml spoons plain flour	*2 teaspoons plain flour*
Salt	*Salt*
Freshly ground pepper	*Freshly ground pepper*

Cooking Time: About 25 to 30 minutes

Put the chicken drumsticks in a shallow dish and cover with the marinade. Leave to marinate for 2 to 4 hours in the refrigerator. Barbecue the drumsticks over glowing charcoal until thoroughly cooked and golden brown.
Meanwhile, put the marinade, stock and tomato purée in a saucepan and bring to the boil. Boil to reduce for 10 minutes. Pour into a jug.
Melt the butter in the rinsed-out saucepan and stir in the flour. Cook, stirring, for 1 minute. Gradually strain in the marinade mixture, stirring. Simmer until thickened. Taste and adjust the seasoning.
Serve the drumsticks with the marinade sauce and Pilaff or Barbecued Baked Potatoes and Corn on the Cob.

Variation:
Use turkey drumsticks and increase cooking time to 35 to 40 minutes.

Barbecued stuffed chicken breasts

Metric	*Imperial*
40 g butter	*$1\frac{1}{2}$ oz butter*
1 small onion, peeled and finely chopped	*1 small onion, peeled and finely chopped*
125 g brown or white rice, washed and dried	*4 oz brown or white rice, washed and dried*
1 × 5 ml spoon turmeric or 1 × 2.5 ml spoon saffron powder	*1 teaspoon turmeric or $\frac{1}{2}$ teaspoon saffron powder*
1 bay leaf	*1 bay leaf*
3 cloves	*3 cloves*
2 cardamom pods	*2 cardamom pods*
Salt	*Salt*
300 ml water	*$\frac{1}{2}$ pint water*
4 chicken breasts, boned	*4 chicken breasts, boned*

Cooking Time: About 40 minutes

Melt the butter in a saucepan and fry the onion with the rice until the onion is transparent. Add the turmeric or saffron, bay leaf, cloves, cardamom and salt to taste. Stir in the water and bring to the boil. Simmer gently until the rice is tender and the water has been absorbed.
Put the chicken breasts between sheets of greaseproof paper and beat until thin. Place a little stuffing on each breast and roll up. Secure with a skewer. Cook over hot charcoal, turning once.
Serve with a green salad and Corn Relish.

Pilaff

Metric	*Imperial*
25 g butter	*1 oz butter*
1 small onion, peeled and finely diced	*1 small onion, peeled and finely diced*
175 g long-grain rice	*6 oz long-grain rice*
450 ml stock or water	*$\frac{3}{4}$ pint stock or water*
Pinch of saffron powder or turmeric	*Pinch of saffron powder or turmeric*
1 × 2.5 ml spoon dried oregano	*$\frac{1}{2}$ teaspoon dried oregano*
Salt	*Salt*
Freshly ground pepper	*Freshly ground pepper*

Cooking Time: 20 to 25 minutes
Oven: 180°C, 350°F, Gas Mark 4

Melt the butter in a saucepan. Add the onion and cook until soft but not brown. Add the rice and cook for 2 to 3 minutes, then stir in the remaining ingredients with salt and pepper to taste. Simmer gently over a low heat on top of the stove or in a preheated moderate oven until the liquid is absorbed and the rice is fluffy and tender. This pilaff is excellent with all skewered food.

Variation:
Omit saffron (for yellow colouring) and add 2 × 15 ml spoons (2 tablespoons) chopped fresh parsley and 1 × 15 ml spoon (1 tablespoon) chopped fresh chives for a green rice.

Barbecued stuffed chicken breasts; Pilaff; Chicken drumstick barbecue

Tandoori turkey

Metric	Imperial
300 ml plain unsweetened yogurt	½ pint plain unsweetened yogurt
1 × 2.5 ml spoon ground ginger	½ teaspoon ground ginger
1 small piece of root ginger, peeled and grated (optional)	1 small piece of root ginger, peeled and grated (optional)
2 × 5 ml spoons paprika	2 teaspoons paprika
1 × 2.5–5 ml spoon chilli powder	½–1 teaspoon chilli powder
1 garlic clove, crushed	1 garlic clove, crushed
4 peppercorns, slightly crushed	4 peppercorns, slightly crushed
1 × 15 ml spoon tomato purée	1 tablespoon tomato purée
1 × 5 ml spoon salt	1 teaspoon salt
Grated rind of 1 lemon	Grated rind of 1 lemon
4 bay leaves	4 bay leaves
Juice of ½ lemon	Juice of ½ lemon
4 turkey joints, skinned	4 turkey joints, skinned
To garnish:	To garnish:
Lemon slices	Lemon slices
Cucumber slices	Cucumber slices

Cooking Time: About 45 minutes to 1¼ hours

Mix together the yogurt, ginger, paprika, chilli powder, garlic, peppercorns, tomato purée, salt, lemon rind, bay leaves and lemon juice. Prick the turkey joints all over with a skewer. Place in a shallow dish with the yogurt marinade, cover and leave to marinate in the refrigerator for at least 24 hours, turning the joints occasionally to ensure that they are well covered.

Remove the bay leaves. Thread the turkey joints onto a long skewer and arrange on bricks about 5 to 7 cm (2 to 3 inches) from a good glowing fire. Turn from time to time and baste with the yogurt marinade during the last 15 minutes of cooking. (Exact cooking time will depend on size of portions.)

Serve garnished with lemon and cucumber slices accompanied by Tomato and Onion Salad, without the French dressing, and Mint Chutney.

Spitted turkey breast

Metric	Imperial
1 × 1–1.75 kg rolled turkey breast	1 × 2–4 lb rolled turkey breast
White Wine Barbecue Marinade (see page 15)	White Wine Barbecue Marinade (see page 15)
Salt	Salt
Freshly ground pepper	Freshly ground pepper

Cooking Time: About 35 to 60 minutes

Place the rolled turkey breast in the marinade and leave to marinate in the refrigerator for 4 to 6 hours, turning occasionally. (Turkey breast is so lean that it really needs the extra moisture added by marinating.) Season well with salt and pepper. Insert the rôtisserie spit carefully into the turkey breast and cook over a good hot fire.

Serve with Barbecued Corn on the Cob and Sweet and Sour Sauce.

Mint chutney

Metric	Imperial
2 spring onions, chopped	2 spring onions, chopped
2 × 15 ml spoons chopped fresh mint	2 tablespoons chopped fresh mint
1 × 2.5 ml spoon salt	½ teaspoon salt
1 × 5 ml spoon sugar	1 teaspoon sugar
1 small chilli, seeded and chopped or large pinch of chilli powder	1 small chilli, seeded and chopped or large pinch of chilli powder
Large pinch of garam masala	Large pinch of garam masala
1 × 15 ml spoon lemon juice	1 tablespoon lemon juice
2 × 15 ml spoons plain unsweetened yogurt (optional)	2 tablespoons plain unsweetened yogurt (optional)

Put all the ingredients, except the lemon juice and yogurt, into a blender or food mill and reduce to a smooth purée. Stir in the lemon juice and yogurt. This chutney will keep for 2 days in the refrigerator, but is better served fresh.

Stuffed mushrooms; Spitted turkey breast; Mint chutney; Tomato and onion salad; Tandoori turkey

Stuffed mushrooms

Metric	*Imperial*
8 large mushrooms	*8 large mushrooms*
2 × 15 ml spoons fresh white breadcrumbs	*2 tablespoons fresh white breadcrumbs*
1 small onion, peeled and finely chopped	*1 small onion, peeled and finely chopped*
1 × 5 ml spoon mixed dried herbs	*1 teaspoon mixed dried herbs*
1 tomato, skinned and chopped	*1 tomato, skinned and chopped*
1 × 15 ml spoon oil	*1 tablespoon oil*

Cooking Time: About 5 minutes

Remove the stalks from the mushrooms and chop finely. Mix the stalks with the breadcrumbs, onion, herbs and tomato. Brush the mushroom caps with oil and arrange on an oiled flameproof plate. Spread each cap with the stuffing and place on the barbecue grid to cook.
Decorate with sprigs of parsley, strips of pimiento or tomato, if liked.

Tomato and onion salad

Metric	*Imperial*
4–6 tomatoes, skinned and thinly sliced	*4–6 tomatoes, skinned and thinly sliced*
2 medium onions, peeled and thinly sliced	*2 medium onions, peeled and thinly sliced*
French dressing (see page 23)	*French dressing (see page 23)*
1 × 5 ml spoon chopped fresh basil or 1 × 2.5 ml spoon dried basil	*1 teaspoon chopped fresh basil or ½ teaspoon dried basil*
2 × 15 ml spoons chopped fresh parsley	*2 tablespoons chopped fresh parsley*

Arrange the tomatoes and onions in a dish and pour over the dressing. Sprinkle the herbs on top.

COOKING ON A SKEWER

Skewered barbecued food is both attractive and easy to eat as everything is in bite-size pieces. And the range of foods you can cook on a skewer is extensive – try sausages, pork, beef, veal, offal, poultry, fish and vegetables.

As skewered food only takes a short time to cook, try to balance it with another barbecued food which takes longer; otherwise it is rather extravagant on charcoal.

Metal skewers are best and they are easy to handle on the barbecue provided you use tongs.

Flat kebab bread, known as pita, is available in many delicatessen shops and is ideal for serving with skewered food. It can be split down one side, filled with shredded lettuce, cucumber, chilli and tomato salad and the kebab meat taken off the skewer and placed inside, Greek style.

An additional advantage of skewered food is that cooking for larger numbers is made easy as all the preparation can be done in advance.

Turkey kebabs; Turkey skewers; Maryland kebabs

Turkey skewers

Metric	*Imperial*
4 × 15 ml spoons oil	*4 tablespoons oil*
1 × 15 ml spoon wine vinegar	*1 tablespoon wine vinegar*
Large pinch of dried oregano	*Large pinch of dried oregano*
1 bay leaf	*1 bay leaf*
Pinch of salt	*Pinch of salt*
Pinch of paprika	*Pinch of paprika*
2 turkey breasts, skinned, boned and cut into squares	*2 turkey breasts, skinned, boned and cut into squares*
1 red pepper, cored, seeded and cut into squares	*1 red pepper, cored, seeded and cut into squares*
8 mushrooms	*8 mushrooms*
8 bay leaves	*8 bay leaves*

Cooking Time: About 20 minutes

Mix together the oil, vinegar, oregano, bay leaf, salt and paprika in a bowl. Add the turkey and turn to coat. Leave to marinate for at least 1 hour.
Thread the squares of turkey, red pepper, whole mushrooms and bay leaves alternately onto skewers. Leave in the marinade for a further 30 minutes.
Place on the barbecue grid and cook, turning and basting frequently.
Serve on a bed of Pilaff with a crisp green salad. Provençale Sauce may be served separately.

Turkey kebabs

Metric	*Imperial*
2 portions turkey breast, skinned, boned and cut into squares	*2 portions turkey breast, skinned, boned and cut into squares*
1 small red pepper, cored, seeded and cut into squares	*1 small red pepper, cored, seeded and cut into squares*
1 small green pepper, cored, seeded and cut into squares	*1 small green pepper, cored, seeded and cut into squares*
100–250 g large prawns, peeled	*4–8 oz large prawns, peeled*
Soured Cream Marinade (see page 14)	*Soured Cream Marinade (see page 14)*

Cooking Time: About 10 to 15 minutes

Put the turkey, red and green peppers and prawns in a shallow dish. Pour over the marinade and turn to coat the ingredients. Leave to marinate for at least 1 hour. Thread the turkey, peppers and prawns alternately onto skewers. Brush well with the marinade and cook over a medium-hot barbecue fire, turning and basting with the marinade from time to time.
Serve on Pilaff with a crisp green salad and spicy Creole Sauce.

Maryland kebabs with mushroom sauce

Metric	*Imperial*
2 chicken breasts, skinned, boned and cut into 3.5 cm pieces	*2 chicken breasts, skinned, boned and cut into 1½ inch pieces*
8 baby onions, peeled or 2 medium onions, peeled	*8 baby onions peeled or 2 medium onions, peeled*
6 streaky bacon rashers, rinds removed	*6 streaky bacon rashers, rinds removed*
3 bananas, peeled and quartered	*3 bananas, peeled and quartered*
1 large red pepper, cored, seeded and cut into 2.5 cm pieces	*1 large red pepper, cored, seeded and cut into 1 inch pieces*
Marinade:	Marinade:
25 g soft brown sugar	*1 oz soft brown sugar*
1 × 15 ml spoon Worcestershire sauce	*1 tablespoon Worcestershire sauce*
2 × 15 ml spoons lemon juice	*2 tablespoons lemon juice*
Large pinch of salt	*Large pinch of salt*

Cooking Time: About 35 minutes

Mix together the ingredients for the marinade in a shallow dish. Add the chicken pieces and turn to coat. Leave to marinate for at least 4 hours in the refrigerator. Parboil the onions in boiling water for 5 minutes. Drain. (If using medium onions, quarter them after boiling.) Stretch the bacon rashers on a board with a round-bladed knife and cut each rasher in half.
Drain the chicken and reserve the marinade. Wrap each piece of banana in a piece of bacon, then dip in the marinade. Thread the chicken, bacon-wrapped bananas, onions and red pepper alternately onto four skewers. Brush with the marinade. Place on the barbecue grid and cook for about 7 minutes. Turn and cook for a further 7 minutes, basting occasionally with the marinade.
Serve on a bed of Pilaff or with Savoury Rice Salad and Mushroom Sauce.

Seafood skewers

Metric

4 streaky bacon rashers
2 cod or halibut steaks, skinned and cut into 8
Salt
Freshly ground pepper
Lemon Marinade (see page 17)
8 large cooked prawns, peeled
4 mushrooms
4 tomatoes, halved

Imperial

4 streaky bacon rashers
2 cod or halibut steaks, skinned and cut into 8
Salt
Freshly ground pepper
Lemon Marinade (see page 17)
8 large cooked prawns, peeled
4 mushrooms
4 tomatoes, halved

Cooking Time: About 8 to 10 minutes

Stretch the bacon rashers on a board with the back of a knife and cut in half. Season the fish pieces with salt and pepper. Roll each piece of fish in a piece of bacon and place in a shallow dish with the marinade. Add the prawns and mushrooms. Leave to marinate in the refrigerator, turning from time to time, for about 4 hours.
Thread the fish, prawns and mushrooms onto skewers with the halved tomatoes, alternating ingredients. Brush well with the marinade and place over a moderately hot barbecue. Cook, turning from time to time. Baste again with marinade towards the end of the cooking time. Serve with Seafood Sauce.

Courgette and tomato skewers

Metric

500 g courgettes, cut into 2 cm thick slices
1 × 15 ml spoon lemon juice
Freshly ground pepper
8 small tomatoes
1 small onion, peeled and sliced
1 × 15 ml spoon oil
Salt

Imperial

1 lb courgettes, cut into $\frac{3}{4}$ inch thick slices
1 tablespoon lemon juice
Freshly ground pepper
8 small tomatoes
1 small onion, peeled and sliced
1 tablespoon oil
Salt

Cooking Time: About 5 to 10 minutes

Blanch the courgette slices in boiling water for 1 minute. Drain well and sprinkle with lemon juice and pepper. Thread the tomatoes, courgettes and onion rings onto skewers and brush with oil. Cook on the barbecue, turning from time to time. Season with salt before serving.

Variation:
Prepare a combination of mixed vegetables and cook as above. Suitable ones are onions, peppers, mushrooms, tomatoes and courgettes.

Barbecued scallops

Metric

8–12 scallops
White Wine Barbecue Marinade (see page 15)
4 tomatoes
4 bay leaves (optional)
25 g butter, melted

Imperial

8–12 scallops
White Wine Barbecue Marinade (see page 15)
4 tomatoes
4 bay leaves (optional)
1 oz butter, melted

Cooking Time: About 5 to 6 minutes

Place the scallops in the marinade and leave to marinate for 2 to 3 hours in the refrigerator. Thread the scallops onto skewers alternately with whole tomatoes and bay leaves, if used. Brush with the melted butter and cook on the barbecue grid, turning and basting with the marinade from time to time. Serve with Stuffed Mushrooms.

Korean kebabs

Metric

1 garlic clove, crushed
4 × 15 ml spoons soy sauce
4 × 15 ml spoons oil
1 × 15 ml spoon peanut butter
2 × 15 ml spoons finely chopped spring onion
1 × 5 ml spoon sesame seeds
Salt
Freshly ground pepper
Pinch of chilli powder
750 g pork, lamb or steak, cut into 1 cm cubes

Imperial

1 garlic clove, crushed
4 tablespoons soy sauce
4 tablespoons oil
1 tablespoon peanut butter
2 tablespoons finely chopped spring onion
1 teaspoon sesame seeds
Salt
Freshly ground pepper
Pinch of chilli powder
$1\frac{1}{2}$ lb pork, lamb or steak, cut into $\frac{1}{2}$ inch cubes

Cooking Time: About 10 to 15 minutes

Put the garlic, soy sauce, oil and peanut butter in a bowl and whisk well. Gradually whisk in the spring onions, sesame seeds, salt and pepper to taste and chilli powder. Add the meat and turn to coat. Leave to marinate for 2 to 4 hours in the refrigerator.
Thread the meat onto small skewers and cook over medium-hot coals. Serve with mustard and Tomato Sauce flavoured with a pinch of chilli powder or a few drops of Tabasco sauce, as an appetizer with drinks. These are very good for winter barbecues or for a Guy Fawkes party, when small Korean Kebabs can be served for adults with mulled wine or cider, and barbecued sausages for the children.

Seafood skewers; Courgette and tomato skewers; Barbecued scallops; Korean kebabs

Somerset barbecue skewers

Metric	*Imperial*
750 g beef shoulder steak, cut into 2.5 cm cubes	*1½ lb beef shoulder steak, cut into 1 inch cubes*
Cider Marinade (see page 36)	*Cider Marinade (see page 36)*
Button mushrooms	*Button mushrooms*
Freshly ground pepper	*Freshly ground pepper*

Cooking Time: About 25 minutes

Put the beef cubes in a shallow dish and pour over the marinade. Leave to marinate in the refrigerator for at least 36 hours. Thread the beef onto skewers, alternating with the button mushrooms, and sprinkle with pepper. Cook over hot charcoal, turning frequently and brushing with the remaining marinade.

Eastern veal skewers

Metric	*Imperial*
1 kg boned leg of veal, cut into 2.5 cm cubes	*2 lb boned leg of veal, cut into 1 inch cubes*
Soured Cream Marinade (see page 14)	*Soured Cream Marinade (see page 14)*
1 aubergine, cut into small cubes	*1 aubergine, cut into small cubes*
Salt	*Salt*
Lemon juice	*Lemon juice*
Freshly ground pepper	*Freshly ground pepper*
12 small onions, peeled	*12 small onions, peeled*
12 bay leaves	*12 bay leaves*

Cooking Time: About 15 minutes

Put the veal cubes in a shallow dish and pour over the marinade. Leave to marinate in the refrigerator for 3 to 4 hours, turning occasionally.

Put the aubergine cubes in a colander and sprinkle with salt. Leave for 30 minutes, then rinse and pat dry with absorbent kitchen paper. Sprinkle the aubergine cubes with more salt, lemon juice and pepper. Blanch the onions in boiling water for 1 to 3 minutes, depending on their size. Drain well.

Thread the skewers alternately with veal, aubergine, onions and bay leaves. Brush with the marinade and cook over the hot coals, turning from time to time.

Spiced rice

Metric	*Imperial*
600 ml water	*1 pint water*
250 g long-grain rice	*8 oz long-grain rice*
1 × 5 ml spoon salt	*1 teaspoon salt*
6 cloves	*6 cloves*
5 cm cinnamon stick	*2 inch cinnamon stick*
1 bay leaf	*1 bay leaf*
4 black peppercorns	*4 black peppercorns*
1 × 2.5 ml spoon saffron powder or tumeric	*½ teaspoon saffron powder or turmeric*
2 × 5 ml spoons milk	*2 teaspoons milk*

Put the water in a saucepan and bring to the boil. Add the rice, salt, cloves, cinnamon stick, bay leaf and peppercorns. Cover and simmer until the rice is tender and all the liquid has been absorbed.

Dissolve the saffron or turmeric in the milk and stir into the rice. Discard the cinnamon stick and bay leaf before serving.

To add colour serve with skinned and sliced tomatoes, sliced cucumber and bananas as a garnish.

Barbecued beef rolls

Metric	*Imperial*
4 minute steaks	*4 minute steaks*
8 small onions, peeled	*8 small onions, peeled*
4 small mushrooms	*4 small mushrooms*
Oriental Marinade (see page 13)	*Oriental Marinade (see page 13)*

Cooking Time: 10 to 15 minutes

Flatten the steaks with a rolling pin. Blanch the onions in boiling water for 2 to 3 minutes. Drain well. Place 2 onions and a mushroom in the centre of each steak and roll the meat around the vegetables. Secure with a skewer. Marinate the steak rolls in the refrigerator for 2 to 3 hours in the Oriental Marinade. Cook the steaks over a hot barbecue, turning from time to time and basting with the remaining marinade.

Serve with Smoky Barbecue Sauce.

Mexican beef kebabs; Eastern veal skewers; Somerset barbecue skewers; Barbecued beef rolls; on a bed of Spiced rice

Mexican beef kebabs

Metric	*Imperial*
4 × 15 ml spoons oil	*4 tablespoons oil*
1 small onion, peeled and chopped	*1 small onion, peeled and chopped*
4 × 15 ml spoons red wine vinegar	*4 tablespoons red wine vinegar*
1 × 2.5 ml spoon salt	*½ teaspoon salt*
1 × 2.5 ml spoon dried oregano	*½ teaspoon dried oregano*
1 × 2.5 ml spoon ground cumin	*½ teaspoon ground cumin*
1 × 2.5 ml spoon ground cloves	*½ teaspoon ground cloves*
1 × 2.5 ml spoon ground cinnamon	*½ teaspoon ground cinnamon*
1 garlic clove, crushed	*1 garlic clove, crushed*
850 g rump steak, cut into 2.5 cm cubes	*1¾ lb rump steak, cut into 1 inch cubes*
Freshly ground pepper	*Freshly ground pepper*
250 g button mushrooms	*8 oz button mushrooms*

Cooking Time: About 12 to 20 minutes

Heat 2 × 15 ml spoons (2 tablespoons) of the oil in a saucepan. Add the onion and cook until golden brown. Stir in the vinegar, salt, oregano, cumin, cloves, cinnamon and garlic. Cover and simmer for 15 to 20 minutes, then allow to cool.

Lay the meat cubes in a dish, brush with the remaining oil and sprinkle with pepper. When the basting sauce has cooled pour over the steak and leave in the refrigerator to marinate for 2 to 4 hours.

Thread the steak cubes onto skewers alternately with the mushrooms. Brush with the marinade and cook over hot glowing charcoal for 12 to 15 minutes for rare steak, 20 minutes for well done. Turn and baste frequently with the marinade.

This beef dish has an excellent flavour and is ideal for entertaining. Serve with Barbecued Baked Potatoes, a tossed green salad, and Courgette and Tomato Skewers.

Sausage and kidney kebabs

Metric	*Imperial*
175 g streaky bacon rashers, rinds removed	*6 oz streaky bacon rashers, rinds removed*
8 chipolata sausages	*8 chipolata sausages*
4 lamb's kidneys, skinned, halved and cored	*4 lamb's kidneys, skinned, halved and cored*
4 small tomatoes	*4 small tomatoes*
2 × 15 ml spoons oil	*2 tablespoons oil*
Salt	*Salt*
Freshly ground pepper	*Freshly ground pepper*

Cooking Time: About 10 minutes

Stretch the bacon rashers with a knife. Cut in half and make into rolls. Twist each sausage and cut into 2 smaller ones. Thread the bacon rolls and sausages onto skewers, alternately with the kidney halves. Finish with a whole tomato. Brush with oil, season with salt and pepper and cook on the barbecue for 5 minutes on each side.
Serve with Creole Sauce.

Pork and apricot kebabs

Metric	*Imperial*
4 small onions, peeled	*4 small onions, peeled*
4 streaky bacon rashers, rinds removed	*4 streaky bacon rashers, rinds removed*
750 g boned leg of pork, cut into 2.5 cm cubes	*1½ lb boned leg of pork, cut into 1 inch cubes*
1 × 225 g can apricot halves, drained	*1 × 8 oz can apricot halves, drained*
8 bay leaves	*8 bay leaves*
Oriental Marinade (see page 13) or oil	*Oriental Marinade (see page 13) or oil*

Cooking Time: 15 minutes

Blanch the onions in boiling water for 4 to 5 minutes and drain. Place the bacon rashers on a board and stretch with the back of a knife. Cut each rasher in half and make into rolls. Thread the pork, onions, bacon rolls, apricot halves and bay leaves onto skewers. Arrange the kebabs in a shallow dish and pour over the marinade. Leave to marinate in the refrigerator for 2 to 4 hours. Alternatively, brush the kebabs with oil and omit the marinating process. Cook over hot coals, turning and brushing with the marinade or oil occasionally. Serve on Pilaff with Smoky Barbecue Sauce.

Pork and apricot kebabs

Mini kebabs

Metric	*Imperial*
750 g shoulder of lamb, cut into 1 cm cubes	*1½ lb shoulder of lamb, cut into ½ inch cubes*
4 tomatoes	*4 tomatoes*
1 red or green pepper, cored, seeded and cut into squares	*1 red or green pepper, cored, seeded and cut into squares*
8 mushrooms	*8 mushrooms*
4 bay leaves	*4 bay leaves*
Marinade:	Marinade:
2 × 15 ml spoons oil	*2 tablespoons oil*
1 × 15 ml spoon wine vinegar	*1 tablespoon wine vinegar*
1 garlic clove, crushed	*1 garlic clove, crushed*
Salt	*Salt*
Freshly ground black pepper	*Freshly ground black pepper*

Cooking Time: About 10 minutes

Mix together the ingredients for the marinade in a polythene bag. Add the lamb cubes and turn to coat. Leave to marinate overnight in the refrigerator.
Thread the lamb cubes onto skewers, alternating with tomatoes, green or red pepper squares, mushrooms and bay leaves. Cook over a hot barbecue, turning occasionally and basting with the marinade.

Liver kebabs; Mini kebabs; Sausage and kidney kebabs

Liver kebabs with onion rings

Metric	*Imperial*
15 g butter or 1 × 15 ml spoon oil	*½ oz butter or 1 tablespoon oil*
375 g lamb's liver, cut into squares	*12 oz lamb's liver, cut into squares*
50 g mushrooms	*2 oz mushrooms*
4 lean bacon rashers, rinds removed, cut into squares	*4 lean bacon rashers, rinds removed, cut into squares*
4 × 15 ml spoons dry breadcrumbs	*4 tablespoons dry breadcrumbs*
Salt	*Salt*
Freshly ground black pepper	*Freshly ground black pepper*
Lemon juice	*Lemon juice*
2 × 15 ml spoons chopped fresh parsley	*2 tablespoons chopped fresh parsley*
1 large onion, peeled and sliced into rings	*1 large onion, peeled and sliced into rings*

Cooking Time: About 15 to 20 minutes

Melt the butter or heat the oil in a frying pan. Add the liver and fry until lightly browned. Remove from the pan. Add the mushrooms and cook for 2 minutes on each side. Remove from the heat. Thread the liver, mushrooms and bacon alternately onto skewers, with a square of liver last. Roll the skewers in the butter or oil used for frying, then in the breadcrumbs. Barbecue for 10 to 12 minutes. Sprinkle with salt, pepper, lemon juice and chopped parsley and serve with onion rings.

Seek kebabs

Metric	Imperial
500 g beef or lamb, finely minced	*1 lb beef or lamb, finely minced*
1 small onion, peeled and grated	*1 small onion, peeled and grated*
1 × 5 ml spoon plain flour	*1 teaspoon plain flour*
1 × 15 ml spoon garam masala	*1 tablespoon garam masala*
Salt	*Salt*
Freshly ground pepper	*Freshly ground pepper*
Pinch of chilli powder	*Pinch of chilli powder*
1 × 5 ml spoon mixed dried herbs or 2 × 5 ml spoons chopped fresh herbs	*1 teaspoon mixed dried herbs or 2 teaspoons chopped fresh herbs*
1 × 15 ml spoon lemon juice	*1 tablespoon lemon juice*
2 × 15 ml spoons plain unsweetened yogurt	*2 tablespoons plain unsweetened yogurt*
1 × 15 ml spoon oil	*1 tablespoon oil*

Cooking Time: About 10 to 15 minutes

Mix together all the ingredients, except the oil, with salt and pepper to taste. (Mint will give a good flavour and can be used as part of the herb mixture.) Divide into 12 portions and shape each into a sausage about 7.5 cm (3 inches) long. Push two sausages, lengthways, onto each of 6 skewers and press on firmly. Chill for 1 hour.
Brush with the oil and cook over a medium hot fire, turning constantly. Serve with Mint Chutney, Tomato and Onion Salad, made without the dressing, and mango chutney.

Souvlakia

Metric	Imperial
1 kg boned leg of lamb, cut into 2.5 cm cubes	*2 lb boned leg of lamb, cut into 1 inch cubes*
2 medium onions, peeled and quartered	*2 medium onions, peeled and quartered*
Juice of 1 lemon	*Juice of 1 lemon*
1 garlic clove, crushed	*1 garlic clove, crushed*
4 × 15 ml spoons oil	*4 tablespoons oil*
Salt	*Salt*
Freshly ground pepper	*Freshly ground pepper*
1 × 5 ml spoon dried oregano	*1 teaspoon dried oregano*
1 × 15 ml spoon chopped fresh parsley	*1 tablespoon chopped fresh parsley*
2 bay leaves	*2 bay leaves*
3 tomatoes, quartered	*3 tomatoes, quartered*

Cooking Time: About 10 to 20 minutes

Lay the lamb cubes in a shallow dish and add the onions. Mix the lemon juice, garlic, oil, salt and pepper to taste and herbs together and pour over the lamb. Allow to marinate in the refrigerator for at least 12 hours.
Thread the lamb onto skewers with the tomatoes and onions and barbecue, turning from time to time.
Serve with Greek bread (pita), heated on the barbecue, wedges of lemon and a pepper, cucumber and lettuce salad.

Variation:
Skewered veal, Greek style, can be made in the same way. Use boned leg of veal and omit the onion. After marinating, thread onto the skewers with whole button mushrooms, if liked.
Serve on Spiced Rice, with Tomato Sauce.

Stuffed peppers

Metric	Imperial
2 medium green peppers, cored, halved lengthways and seeded	*2 medium green peppers, cored, halved lengthways and seeded*
225 g lean minced beef	*8 oz lean minced beef*
1 celery stalk, finely chopped	*1 celery stalk, finely chopped*
1 small onion, peeled and finely chopped	*1 small onion, peeled and finely chopped*
150 ml Tomato Sauce (see page 19)	*¼ pint Tomato Sauce (see page 19)*
Salt	*Salt*
Freshly ground pepper	*Freshly ground pepper*
1 × 2.5 ml spoon dried oregano	*½ teaspoon dried oregano*
Oil	*Oil*

Cooking Time: 1 hour

Blanch the peppers in boiling water for 2 minutes. Drain. Brown the meat in a frying pan with the celery and onion. Add the tomato sauce, salt and pepper to taste and the oregano and mix well. Stuff the peppers with the meat mixture and brush the skins with oil. Cook, cut sides up, on the side of the barbecue.
Serve as a starter, or as an accompaniment to barbecued food.

Seek kebabs; Sosaties; Souvlakia; Stuffed peppers

Sosaties

Metric	*Imperial*
1 × 1.25 kg leg of lamb	*1 × 2¾ lb leg of lamb*
4 medium onions, peeled and sliced	*4 medium onions, peeled and sliced*
150 ml malt vinegar	*¼ pint malt vinegar*
1 × 15 ml spoon curry powder	*1 tablespoon curry powder*
1 × 15 ml spoon turmeric	*1 tablespoon turmeric*
2 × 5 ml spoons salt	*2 teaspoons salt*
6 black peppercorns, slightly crushed	*6 black peppercorns, slightly crushed*
8 allspice berries	*8 allspice berries*
5 cm cinnamon stick	*2 inch cinnamon stick*
3 bay leaves	*3 bay leaves*
2 × 15 ml spoons apricot jam	*2 tablespoons apricot jam*
1 cooking apple, peeled, cored and chopped	*1 cooking apple, peeled, cored and chopped*

Cooking Time: About 15 to 20 minutes

Trim excess fat from the leg of lamb. Stand on its side and cut in 2.5 cm (1 inch) thick slices to the bone. Cut into cubes.

Put the onions in a saucepan and just cover with water. Bring to the boil and simmer until the onions are opaque and the water has evaporated completely. Add the vinegar, curry powder, turmeric, salt, peppercorns, allspice and cinnamon. Return to the boil and stir in the bay leaves, jam and apple. Remove from the heat and cool completely.

Thread the meat onto skewers. Place the sauce and skewered meat in layers in a deep dish. Allow to marinate for 2 to 3 days in the refrigerator. Cook over hot coals until tender. The marinade may be reduced and strained to make a sauce.

Serves 8

PICNIC FOODS

Picnic meals range from the exotic to the simple sandwich, but whatever the occasion do keep the suggestions given in the introduction in mind to make every picnic successful.

Cold meats and salads are easily carried in plastic boxes. Dressings and mayonnaise can be transported in plastic tumblers with rigid lids, or in screw-topped jars.

The pies and quiches in this section are all ideal picnic food and are easily carried if repacked in the tin or flan ring in which they were cooked and covered with foil or cling film. Everything should be in one piece when you arrive at the picnic site. Pies, flans and cakes remain more moist if packed whole; but for a short journey or garden picnic they can be cut into slices. With a fruit cake it is easier to pack slices in foil or cling film, unless the whole cake is going to be eaten.

Fresh fruit with a slice of cake makes an excellent picnic dessert. Strawberries, raspberries or other fresh fruit can be packed in plastic sweet dishes with lids. Cream can be taken if you have a cold box.

The sweets in this section are all easily carried, but do beware of soft creamy desserts which will not travel intact or survive the heat of the day. Elaborate desserts are best served from the kitchen at garden picnics or barbecues when the refrigerator can be used to keep them in prime condition.

Tuna pâté

Metric

100 g butter, melted
2 garlic cloves, crushed
2 × 200 g cans tuna fish, drained
2 × 15 ml spoons olive oil
1 × 15 ml spoon lemon juice
Salt
Freshly ground pepper
Chopped parsley, to garnish

Imperial

4 oz butter, melted
2 garlic cloves, crushed
2 × 7 oz cans tuna fish, drained
2 tablespoons olive oil
1 tablespoon lemon juice
Salt
Freshly ground pepper
Chopped parsley, to garnish

Mix together the butter and garlic. Roughly flake the tuna fish and place half in a blender goblet with half the melted butter mixture and 1 × 15 ml spoon (1 tablespoon) of the olive oil. Blend until smooth. Remove and blend the remaining fish with the remaining butter mixture and olive oil. Mix all the blended fish together and stir in the lemon juice and salt and pepper to taste. Spoon into a serving dish and garnish with chopped parsley. Cover with foil or cling film and chill.

Serves 8

Taramasalata

Metric

1 slice of white bread, crusts removed
4 × 15 ml spoons olive oil
1–2 garlic cloves
225 g smoked cod's roe
1 small potato, cooked and peeled
Lemon juice
2–3 fresh parsley sprigs
2 × 15 ml spoons cold water
Salt
Freshly ground pepper

To garnish:
Lemon wedges
Black olives

Imperial

1 slice of white bread, crusts removed
4 tablespoons olive oil
1–2 garlic cloves
8 oz smoked cod's roe
1 small potato, cooked and peeled
Lemon juice
2–3 fresh parsley sprigs
2 tablespoons cold water
Salt
Freshly ground pepper

To garnish:
Lemon wedges
Black olives

Soak the bread in cold water. Squeeze dry. Pour the oil into a blender goblet and add the garlic, cod's roe, potato, lemon juice to taste, bread and parsley. Blend until smooth. (A better consistency is obtained if the ingredients are added a little at a time.) Thin with a little of the cold water if the mixture seems too stiff to blend. Add salt and pepper to taste, then stir in the remaining water to give a soft, creamy consistency. Pour into a bowl or rigid plastic box and smooth the top. Cover with foil or cling film and chill. Serve garnished with lemon wedges and black olives, accompanied by Greek bread (pita).

Serves 6

Taramasalata; Tuna pâté

Turkey and pork pâté; Terrine of rabbit; Chicken mousse; Country chicken liver pâté

Chicken mousse

Metric	*Imperial*
25 g aspic jelly	*1 oz aspic jelly*
350 g cooked chicken	*12 oz cooked chicken*
300 ml milk	*½ pint milk*
1 bay leaf	*1 bay leaf*
½ carrot, peeled and sliced	*½ carrot, peeled and sliced*
½ onion, peeled and sliced	*½ onion, peeled and sliced*
6 peppercorns	*6 peppercorns*
50 g margarine	*2 oz margarine*
50 g plain flour	*2 oz plain flour*
4 × 15 ml spoons mayonnaise	*4 tablespoons mayonnaise*
2 × 15 ml spoons medium sherry	*2 tablespoons medium sherry*
Salt	*Salt*
Freshly ground black pepper	*Freshly ground black pepper*
300 ml whipping cream	*½ pint whipping cream*
Cucumber slices, to garnish	*Cucumber slices, to garnish*

Make up the aspic jelly to 150 ml (¼ pint) as directed on the packet. Mince the chicken twice using a fine mincer attachment. Bring the milk to the boil in a saucepan with the bay leaf, carrot, onion and peppercorns. Remove from the heat and allow to infuse for 10 minutes. Strain. Melt the margarine in the rinsed-out saucepan. Add the flour and cook, stirring, for 1 minute. Gradually stir in the milk and bring to the boil, stirring. Simmer until smooth and thickened. Remove from the heat and allow to cool.

Stir the mayonnaise, chicken, sherry and half the aspic jelly into the cooled sauce. Mix well together and season to taste with salt and pepper. Lightly whip the cream and fold into the mixture.

Spoon into a 15 cm (6 inch) diameter soufflé dish and chill until set. Garnish with cucumber slices and pour on the cool, but not yet set, remaining aspic jelly. Chill until set, then cover with foil or cling film.

Terrine of rabbit

Metric	Imperial
6 streaky bacon rashers, rinds removed	6 streaky bacon rashers, rinds removed
750 g cooked rabbit	1½ lb cooked rabbit
750 g fat pork, finely minced	1½ lb fat pork, finely minced
2 × 15 ml spoons brandy	2 tablespoons brandy
2 garlic cloves, crushed	2 garlic cloves, crushed
1 × 5 ml spoon dried thyme	1 teaspoon dried thyme
Salt	Salt
Freshly ground black pepper	Freshly ground black pepper

Cooking Time: 1¼ hours
Oven: 180°C, 350°F, Gas Mark 4

Stretch the bacon rashers using the flat of a knife blade. Use to line a 500 g (1 lb) loaf tin (22 × 11 × 6 cm/8½ × 4½ × 2½ inch). Remove the rabbit meat from the bones and mince finely. Add to the minced pork and mix well. Stir in the brandy, garlic, thyme and salt and pepper to taste. Spoon the meat mixture into the bacon-lined tin and smooth the surface.
Cover with foil and place the tin in a roasting tin half filled with water. Bake in a preheated moderate oven. Remove from the oven and place heavy weights on top of the terrine until cold and set firmly. Cover with foil, or cut in slices and wrap in foil.
Serves 6 to 8

Turkey and pork pâté

Metric	Imperial
275 g turkey meat	10 oz turkey meat
225 g lean pork	8 oz lean pork
225 g chicken livers	8 oz chicken livers
3 × 15 ml spoons dry white wine	3 tablespoons dry white wine
2 garlic cloves, crushed	2 garlic cloves, crushed
1 × 5 ml spoon dried thyme	1 teaspoon dried thyme
40 g fresh white breadcrumbs	1½ oz fresh white breadcrumbs
Salt	Salt
Freshly ground black pepper	Freshly ground black pepper
4 bay leaves	4 bay leaves
6 streaky bacon rashers	6 streaky bacon rashers

Cooking Time: 1½ hours
Oven: 180°C, 350°F, Gas Mark 4

Put the turkey, pork and chicken livers twice through a mincer fitted with a fine cutter. Stir in the white wine, garlic, thyme and breadcrumbs. Season well with salt and pepper. Arrange the bay leaves diagonally along the bottom of a 500 g (1 lb) loaf tin (22 × 11 × 6 cm/8½ × 4½ × 2½ inches). Stretch the bacon rashers using the back of a knife blade. Line the tin with the rashers. Spoon the meat mixture into the lined tin.
Cover with foil and place in a roasting tin half filled with water. Bake in a preheated moderate oven. Allow to cool in the tin, then place weights over the surface and leave until firmly set. Cover with foil. Alternatively slice thickly and wrap the slices in foil.
Serves 8

Country chicken liver pâté

Metric	Imperial
150 g butter	5 oz butter
½ onion, peeled and chopped	½ onion, peeled and chopped
225 g chicken livers, roughly chopped	8 oz chicken livers, roughly chopped
225 g pig's liver, skinned and roughly chopped	8 oz pig's liver, skinned and roughly chopped
1 × 5 ml spoon dried thyme	1 teaspoon dried thyme
1 bay leaf	1 bay leaf
Salt	Salt
Freshly ground black pepper	Freshly ground black pepper
150 ml chicken stock	¼ pint chicken stock
1 × 15 ml spoon brandy	1 tablespoon brandy

Melt 75 g (3 oz) of the butter in a pan and cook the onion until it is soft. Add the chicken and pig's liver and seal quickly, stirring frequently to prevent sticking. Add the thyme, bay leaf and salt and pepper to taste, then stir in the stock. Bring to the boil, cover and simmer for 15 minutes. Remove from the heat and allow to cool slightly.
Put the liver mixture in a blender goblet with 4 × 15 ml spoons (4 tablespoons) of the liquid in the pan and blend until smooth, adding more liquid if required. Stir in the brandy, taste and adjust seasoning and spoon into a dish or plastic box. Allow to cool.
Melt the remaining butter in a saucepan over very low heat. Skim the foam from the top, then strain the clear yellow liquid into a bowl, leaving any milky residue in the pan. Allow to cool slightly, then pour over the pâté. Allow to set in the refrigerator and cover with foil to carry.
Serves 6 to 8

Raised pork pie

Raised pork pie

Metric	*Imperial*
500 g veal and pork bones	*1 lb veal and pork bones*
225 g chopped mixed vegetables (onion, carrot, celery, leek)	*8 oz chopped mixed vegetables (onion, carrot, celery, leek)*
1 bay leaf	*1 bay leaf*
Salt	*Salt*
Freshly ground black pepper	*Freshly ground black pepper*
1 kg lean pork, cut into 1 cm cubes	*2 lb lean pork, cut into ½ inch cubes*
2 × 15 ml spoons chopped fresh parsley	*2 tablespoons chopped fresh parsley*
Hot-water crust pastry:	Hot-water crust pastry:
450 g plain flour	*1 lb plain flour*
2 × 5 ml spoons salt	*2 teaspoons salt*
100 g lard	*4 oz lard*
120 ml milk	*4 fl oz milk*
120 ml water	*4 fl oz water*
Beaten egg to glaze	*Beaten egg to glaze*

Cooking Time: 2 hours
Oven: 200°C, 400°F, Gas Mark 6
180°C, 350°F, Gas Mark 4

Put the veal and pork bones and vegetables in a large pan and cover with water. Add the bay leaf, salt and pepper. Bring to the boil, cover and simmer for 1½ hours. Strain and return to the pan. Boil until reduced to 300 ml (½ pint). Allow to cool, then chill until set and jellied.
Mix the cubed pork with the parsley and season well.
For the pastry sift the flour and salt into a bowl. Heat the lard, milk and water in a saucepan over a low heat until the lard has melted; do not boil. Add this mixture to the flour and mix well. Roll out two-thirds of the dough into a circle and use to line a 15 cm (6 inch) loose-bottomed cake tin, leaving the dough overlapping the tin edge. Spoon the pork mixture into the lined tin.
Roll out the remaining dough to a circle. Dampen the edges with water and cover the pie, sealing the edges well together. Use the trimmings to make leaves to decorate the top. Make a ventilation hole in the centre. Glaze with beaten egg and bake in the centre of a preheated moderately hot oven for 30 minutes. Reduce the heat to moderate and bake for a further 1½ hours. Leave to cool.
Bring the jellied stock to just below boiling point and allow to cool. Pour through the hole in the lid of the pie, using a funnel. Leave to set, then remove from the tin and wrap in foil or carry in the tin.
Serves 6

Raised savoury pie

Raised savoury pie

Metric

625 g quantity hot-water crust pastry dough, made with 625 g plain flour, salt, 125 g lard, 150 ml milk and 150 ml water (see opposite)
Beaten egg to glaze
300 ml well-seasoned jellied veal and pork bone stock (see opposite)

Filling:
1 × 1.5 kg oven-ready chicken
500 g lean pork, finely minced
1 onion, peeled and minced
225 g lean streaky bacon, rinds removed, minced
2 × 15 ml spoons chopped fresh parsley
1 × 2.5 ml spoon dried sage
Salt
Freshly ground black pepper
225 g pork sausagemeat

Imperial

1¼ lb quantity hot-water crust pastry dough, made with 1¼ lb plain flour, salt, 5 oz lard, ¼ pint milk and ¼ pint water (see opposite)
Beaten egg to glaze
½ pint well-seasoned jellied veal and pork bone stock (see opposite)

Filling:
1 × 3 lb oven-ready chicken
1 lb lean pork, finely minced
1 onion, peeled and minced
8 oz lean streaky bacon, rinds removed, minced
2 tablespoons chopped fresh parsley
½ teaspoon dried sage
Salt
Freshly ground black pepper
8 oz pork sausagemeat

Cooking Time: 2½ hours
Oven: 200°C, 400°F, Gas Mark 6
180°C, 350°F, Gas Mark 4

Remove the chicken meat from the bones and skin. Cut the breasts into pieces. Mince the rest of the meat and add to the pork, onion and bacon. Stir in the parsley, sage and salt and pepper to taste.
Roll out two-thirds of the dough to a circle and use to line an 18 cm (7 inch) loose-bottomed cake tin, leaving the dough overlapping the edge. Spread half the sausagemeat over the pastry base and spoon half the meat filling on top. Cover with the chicken breast pieces and top with the remaining meat mixture. Cover with the rest of the sausagemeat.
Roll out the remaining dough to a circle. Dampen the edges with water and cover the pie, sealing the edges well together. Decorate with the pastry trimmings. Make a hole in the centre of the pie. Brush with beaten egg and bake in a preheated moderately hot oven for 30 minutes. Reduce the heat to moderate and bake a further 2 hours. Allow to cool.
Bring the jellied stock to just below boiling point and allow to cool. Pour through the hole in the lid of the pie, using a funnel. Leave to set, then remove from the tin and wrap in foil or carry in the tin.
Serves 6 to 8

Bacon and corn quiche; Spinach and mushroom quiche; Raised game pie

Bacon and corn quiche

Metric	*Imperial*
Shortcrust pastry:	Shortcrust pastry:
175 g plain flour	*6 oz plain flour*
Pinch of salt	*Pinch of salt*
75 g mixed margarine and lard	*3 oz mixed margarine and lard*
1–2 × 15 ml spoons cold water	*1–2 tablespoons cold water*
Filling:	Filling:
15 g margarine	*½ oz margarine*
6 streaky bacon rashers, rinds removed, chopped	*6 streaky bacon rashers, rinds removed, chopped*
1 small onion, peeled and finely chopped	*1 small onion, peeled and finely chopped*
1 × 200 g can sweetcorn, drained	*1 × 7 oz can sweetcorn, drained*
2 eggs	*2 eggs*
200 ml milk	*⅓ pint milk*
1 × 5 ml spoon dried thyme	*1 teaspoon dried thyme*
Salt	*Salt*
Freshly ground black pepper	*Freshly ground black pepper*

Cooking Time: 35 minutes
Oven: 200°C, 400°F, Gas Mark 6
180°C, 350°F, Gas Mark 4

To make the pastry, sift the flour and salt into a mixing bowl. Cut in the margarine and lard, then rub in until the mixture resembles breadcrumbs. Bind together with the water to form a dough. Leave to rest for 10 minutes.

Roll out the dough and use to line a 23 cm (9 inch) loose-bottomed flan ring. Place a piece of greeaseproof paper on the pastry, then fill with baking beans. Bake in a preheated moderately hot oven for 10 minutes. Remove the paper and beans and bake for a further 10 minutes. Allow to cool.

Melt the margarine in a frying pan and fry the bacon and onion until soft. Drain and place in the cooked flan case. Cover with the sweetcorn. Beat the eggs and add the milk, herbs and salt and pepper to taste. Pour over the bacon and corn mixture. Bake in a preheated moderately hot oven for 10 minutes. Reduce the heat to moderate and bake for a further 25 minutes. Leave in flan ring for easy carrying and cover with cling film or foil.

Serves 6

Raised game pie

Metric	*Imperial*
625 g quantity hot-water crust pastry dough, made with 625 g plain flour, 125 g lard, 150 ml milk and 150 ml water (see page 64)	*1¼ lb quantity hot-water crust pastry dough, made with 1¼ lb plain flour, 5 oz lard, ¼ pint milk and ¼ pint water (see page 64)*
Beaten egg to glaze	*Beaten egg to glaze*
300 ml well-seasoned jellied veal and pork bone stock (see page 64)	*½ pint well-seasoned jellied veal and pork bone stock (see page 64)*
Filling:	Filling:
350 g pheasant meat, chopped or minced	*12 oz pheasant meat, chopped or minced*
350 g chicken meat, chopped or minced	*12 oz chicken meat, chopped or minced*
350 g fat pork, chopped or minced	*12 oz fat pork, chopped or minced*
3–4 × 15 ml spoons brandy	*3–4 tablespoons brandy*
1 × 5 ml spoon dried mixed herbs	*1 teaspoon dried mixed herbs*
Salt	*Salt*
Freshly ground black pepper	*Freshly ground black pepper*
6 streaky bacon rashers, rinds removed, stretched and halved	*6 streaky bacon rashers, rinds removed, stretched and halved*

Cooking Time: 2½ hours
Oven: 200°C, 400°F, Gas Mark 6
180°C, 350°F, Gas Mark 4

Mix together the pheasant and chicken meat and fat pork. Stir in the brandy, mixed herbs and salt and pepper to taste. Roll out two-thirds of the dough and use to line an 18 cm (7 inch) loose-bottomed cake tin, leaving the dough overlapping the tin edge. Spoon half the pheasant mixture into the lined tin and cover with half the bacon rashers. Top with the remaining meat mixture and the rest of the bacon. Roll out the remaining dough to a circle. Dampen the edges with water and cover the pie, sealing the edges well together. Decorate with the pastry trimmings. Make a hole in the centre of the pie. Glaze with beaten egg. Bake in the centre of a preheated moderately hot oven for 30 minutes. Reduce the temperature to moderate, cover with foil and cook for a further 2 hours. Leave to cool.
Bring the jellied stock to just below boiling point and allow to cool. Pour through the hole in the lid of the pie, using a funnel. Leave to set, then remove from the tin and wrap in foil or carry in the tin.
Serves 6

Variation:
The pheasant and chicken can be partially cooked first, removed from the bones and placed in the pie in slices.

Spinach and mushroom quiche

Metric	*Imperial*
Rich shortcrust pastry:	Rich shortcrust pastry:
175 g plain flour	*6 oz plain flour*
Pinch of salt	*Pinch of salt*
125 g hard margarine or butter	*4 oz hard margarine or butter*
1 egg yolk	*1 egg yolk*
1 × 15 ml spoon cold water	*1 tablespoon cold water*
Filling:	Filling:
225 g frozen chopped spinach	*8 oz frozen chopped spinach*
25 g butter	*1 oz butter*
1 small onion, peeled and diced	*1 small onion, peeled and diced*
125 g mushrooms, sliced	*4 oz mushrooms, sliced*
3 eggs	*3 eggs*
150 ml double cream	*¼ pint double cream*
Salt	*Salt*
Freshly ground black pepper	*Freshly ground black pepper*
Large pinch of dried basil	*Large pinch of dried basil*

Cooking Time: 40 to 50 minutes
Oven: 200°C, 400°F, Gas Mark 6
180°C, 350°F, Gas Mark 4

To make the pastry, sift the flour and salt into a mixing bowl. Cut in the margarine or butter, then rub in until the mixture resembles breadcrumbs. Bind together with the egg yolk and water to form a dough. Chill for 20 minutes. Roll out the dough and use to line a 23 cm (9 inch) loose-bottomed flan ring. Place a piece of greaseproof paper on the pastry, then fill with baking beans. Bake in a preheated moderately hot oven for 15 minutes. Remove the paper and beans and bake for a further 5 minutes. Allow to cool.
Cook the spinach according to the directions on the packet. Drain well.
Melt the butter in a frying pan. Add the onion and fry until soft but not brown. Stir in the mushrooms and cook for 2 minutes. Remove from the heat and stir in the spinach. Spoon into the pastry case, reserving a few slices of mushroom to garnish.
Beat the eggs and cream together and season well with salt and pepper and the basil. Pour into the pastry case. Decorate with the reserved mushroom slices and bake in a preheated moderate oven for 20 to 30 minutes or until just set. Allow to cool, then cover with cling film and chill in the refrigerator until the last moment. Place in a rigid container for easy carrying or leave in the tin.
Serves 6 to 8

Curried chicken tartlets

Metric	*Imperial*
175 g quantity rich short-crust pastry (see page 67)	*6 oz quantity rich short-crust pastry (see page 67)*
2 × 5 ml spoons curry powder	*2 teaspoons curry powder*
2 × 15 ml spoons lemon juice	*2 tablespoons lemon juice*
100 g walnuts, roughly chopped	*4 oz walnuts, roughly chopped*
350 g cooked chicken meat, cut into thin strips	*12 oz cooked chicken meat, cut into thin strips*
120–150 ml mayonnaise	*4–5 fl oz (¼ pint) mayonnaise*
Salt	*Salt*
Freshly ground black pepper	*Freshly ground black pepper*
Chopped fresh parsley	*Chopped fresh parsley*

Cooking Time: 15 minutes
Oven: 200°C, 400°F, Gas Mark 6

Divide the pastry dough into four. Roll out each piece and use to line four 11.5 cm (4½ inch) diameter tartlet cases. Bake blind for 15 minutes (see page 67) and allow to cool. Stir the curry powder, lemon juice, walnuts and chicken into the mayonnaise and season to taste with salt and pepper. Spoon into the tartlet cases and sprinkle with chopped parsley. Cover with cling film and store in refrigerator until last moment. Place in a rigid plastic container for easy carrying.

Welsh picnic flans

Metric	*Imperial*
500 g quantity rich short-crust pastry dough, made with 500 g plain flour, pinch of salt, 350 g hard butter or margarine, 2 egg yolks and 3 × 15 ml spoons water (see page 67)	*1 lb quantity rich short-crust pastry dough, made with 1 lb plain flour, pinch of salt, 12 oz hard butter or margarine, 2 egg yolks and 3 tablespoons water (see page 67)*
50 g butter	*2 oz butter*
5 large leeks, sliced	*5 large leeks, sliced*
1 × 5 ml spoon dried oregano	*1 teaspoon dried oregano*
5 eggs	*5 eggs*
300 ml single cream	*½ pint single cream*
Salt	*Salt*
Freshly ground pepper	*Freshly ground pepper*
1 × 15 ml spoon chopped fresh parsley	*1 tablespoon chopped fresh parsley*

Cooking Time: About 20 minutes
Oven: 180°C, 350°F, Gas Mark 4

Roll out the pastry dough and use to line six 11.5 cm (4½ inch) diameter flan rings and one 20 cm (8 inch) diameter flan ring. Bake blind for 20 minutes (see page 67) and allow to cool. Melt the butter in a frying pan. Add the leeks and fry gently until transparent. Remove from the heat and allow to cool. Sprinkle over the oregano and divide between the pastry shells. Beat together the eggs, cream and salt and pepper to taste and pour over the leeks. Sprinkle with the chopped parsley. Bake in a preheated moderate oven for 20 minutes. Allow to cool, then cover individual flans with cling film and place in rigid containers for easy carrying.
Serves 10 to 12

Variation:
Sprinkle grated Parmesan cheese over the flans before cooking.

Welsh picnic flans; Curried chicken tartlets; Crab and cheese flan

Crab and cheese flan

Metric	*Imperial*
1 × 200 g can crab meat, drained and flaked	*1 × 7 oz can crab meat, drained and flaked*
*1 × 23 cm baked rich shortcrust pastry flan case (see page **67**)*	*1 × 9 inch baked rich shortcrust pastry flan case (see page **67**)*
2 eggs	*2 eggs*
200 ml milk	*⅓ pint milk*
75 g Cheddar cheese, finely grated	*3 oz Cheddar cheese, finely grated*
Salt	*Salt*
Freshly ground black pepper	*Freshly ground black pepper*

Cooking Time: 35 minutes
Oven: 200°C, 400°F, Gas Mark 6
180°C, 350°F, Gas Mark 4

Put the crab meat in the pastry case. Beat the eggs together and add the milk and grated cheese. Season well with salt and pepper and pour over the crab meat. Bake in a preheated moderately hot oven for 10 minutes, then reduce the heat to moderate and cook for a further 25 minutes. Allow to cool, then cover with foil or cling film.
Serves 6

Chicken and asparagus flan

Metric	*Imperial*
175–225 g cooked chicken meat, diced	*6–8 oz cooked chicken meat, diced*
1 × 23 cm baked rich shortcrust pastry flan case (see page 67)	*1 × 9 inch baked rich shortcrust pastry flan case (see page 67)*
1 × 325 g can asparagus, drained	*1 × 11½ oz can asparagus, drained*
2 eggs	*2 eggs*
200 ml single cream	*⅓ pint single cream*
Salt	*Salt*
Freshly ground pepper	*Freshly ground pepper*

Cooking Time: 30 minutes
Oven: 200°C, 400°F, Gas Mark 6
160°C, 325°F, Gas Mark 3

Put the chicken in the pastry case and arrange the asparagus on top. Beat the eggs and add the cream and salt and pepper to taste. Pour into the pastry case and bake in a preheated moderately hot oven for 10 minutes. Reduce the heat to moderate and bake for a further 25 to 30 minutes. Allow to cool, then cover with aluminium foil or cling film.
Serves 6

Pâté chicken pie

Metric	*Imperial*
1 × 1.5 kg chicken	*1 × 3 lb chicken*
1 large carrot, peeled and sliced	*1 large carrot, peeled and sliced*
1 onion, peeled and sliced	*1 onion, peeled and sliced*
Salt	*Salt*
Freshly ground pepper	*Freshly ground pepper*
900 ml water	*1½ pints water*
25 g margarine	*1 oz margarine*
25 g plain flour	*1 oz plain flour*
1 × 5 ml spoon dried rosemary	*1 teaspoon dried rosemary*
275 g quantity shortcrust pastry dough, made with 275 g plain flour, pinch of salt, 150 g mixed margarine and lard, and 3–4 × 15 ml spoons cold water (see page 66)	*10 oz quantity shortcrust pastry dough, made with 10 oz plain flour, pinch of salt, 5 oz mixed margarine and lard, and 3–4 tablespoons cold water (see page 66)*
175 g liver sausage, sliced	*6 oz liver sausage, sliced*
2 large tomatoes, sliced	*2 large tomatoes, sliced*
Beaten egg to glaze	*Beaten egg to glaze*

Cooking Time: 2¼ hours
Oven: 200°C, 400°F, Gas Mark 6

Put the chicken, carrot, onion and salt and pepper in a saucepan. Add the water and bring to the boil. Cover and simmer for 1¼ hours. Strain off the stock and retain 300 ml (½ pint). Skin the chicken and cut the meat into slices.
Melt the margarine in a saucepan. Stir in the flour and cook for 2 minutes. Remove from the heat and gradually stir in the reserved stock. Return to the heat and bring to the boil. Simmer for 2 to 3 minutes. Season with salt and pepper and stir in the rosemary. Add the chicken meat and allow to cool.
Roll out two thirds of the dough and use to line a 20 cm (8 inch) loose-bottomed cake tin. Line the pastry base with the slices of liver sausage. Pour over the chicken sauce and top with the slices of tomato. Roll out the remaining dough and use to cover the pie. Decorate with the pastry trimmings. Brush with beaten egg. Bake in a preheated moderately hot oven for about 1 hour, covering with foil if the pastry browns too rapidly. Allow to cool, then cover with foil or remove from the tin and wrap in foil.
Serves 4 to 6

Mushroom quiche

Metric	*Imperial*
15 g butter or margarine	*½ oz butter or margarine*
1 small onion, peeled and chopped	*1 small onion, peeled and chopped*
175 g mushrooms, chopped	*6 oz mushrooms, chopped*
1 × 5 ml spoon lemon juice	*1 teaspoon lemon juice*
1 × 23 cm baked shortcrust pastry flan case (see page 66)	*1 × 9 inch baked shortcrust pastry flan case (see page 66)*
75 g cheese, grated	*3 oz cheese, grated*
2 eggs	*2 eggs*
200 ml milk	*⅓ pint milk*
1 × 5 ml spoon dried mixed herbs	*1 teaspoon dried mixed herbs*
Salt	*Salt*
Freshly ground pepper	*Freshly ground pepper*

Cooking Time: 35 minutes
Oven: 200°C, 400°F, Gas Mark 6
180°C, 350°F, Gas Mark 4

Melt the butter or margarine in a frying pan. Add the onion and fry until soft. Add the mushrooms and lemon juice and cook for 2 minutes. Drain the vegetables and spread in the flan case. Sprinkle the grated cheese on top.
Beat the eggs together and add the milk, herbs and salt and pepper to taste. Pour into the flan case. Bake in a preheated moderately hot oven for 10 minutes, then reduce the heat to moderate and bake for a further 25 minutes. Allow to cool, then cover with cling film.
Serves 6

Chicken and asparagus flan; Mushroom quiche; Pâté chicken pie

Burgundy beef pies

Metric

3 × 15 ml spoons oil
500 g lean chuck steak, cut into 1 cm cubes
1 medium onion, peeled and finely chopped
150 ml beef stock
150 ml Burgundy red wine
1 × 5 ml spoon dried marjoram
1 bay leaf
Salt
Freshly ground black pepper
1 × 15 ml spoon cornflour
2 × 15 ml spoons cold water
100 g button mushrooms, roughly chopped
350 g quantity rich short-crust pastry dough, made with 350 g plain flour, pinch of salt, 225 g hard margarine or butter, 2 egg yolks and 2 × 15 ml spoons cold water (see page 67)
Beaten egg to glaze

Imperial

3 tablespoons oil
1 lb lean chuck steak, cut into $\frac{1}{2}$ inch cubes
1 medium onion, peeled and finely chopped
$\frac{1}{4}$ pint beef stock
$\frac{1}{4}$ pint Burgundy red wine
1 teaspoon dried marjoram
1 bay leaf
Salt
Freshly ground black pepper
1 tablespoon cornflour
2 tablespoons cold water
4 oz button mushrooms, roughly chopped
12 oz quantity rich short-crust pastry dough, made with 12 oz plain flour, pinch of salt, 8 oz hard margarine or butter, 2 egg yolks and 2 tablespoons cold water (see page 67)
Beaten egg to glaze

Cooking Time: 2 hours
Oven: 220°C, 425°F, Gas Mark 7
180°C, 350°F, Gas Mark 4

Heat the oil in a saucepan. Add the steak cubes and brown quickly on all sides. Remove from the pan with a slotted spoon. Add the onion to the pan and fry until soft. Return the meat to the pan with the stock, red wine, marjoram, bay leaf and salt and pepper to taste. Bring to the boil, cover and simmer for $1\frac{1}{2}$ hours.

Dissolve the cornflour in the water and stir into the beef. Simmer until thickened. Add the mushrooms and allow to cool.

Divide the dough in half. Roll out one half and cut out eight circles slightly larger than the diameter of eight Yorkshire pudding tins. Use to line the tins. Divide the beef and mushroom mixture between the tins. Roll out the remaining dough and cut out eight circles for the lids. Dampen the edges of the pastry with water and press the lids on well over the meat filling. Make a hole in the centres of the lids. Glaze with beaten egg and bake near the top of a preheated hot oven for 15 minutes. Reduce the heat to moderate and bake for a further 15 minutes. Allow to cool.

Place pies in a rigid plastic container with a tight fitting lid, or leave in the tins and cover with foil.

Makes 8 pies

Cornish pasties

Metric

350 g lean chuck steak, cut into 1 cm pieces
$\frac{1}{2}$ medium onion, peeled and finely chopped
1 × 5 ml spoon dried marjoram
100 g potato, peeled and diced
2–3 × 5 ml spoons prepared French mustard
50 g mushrooms, finely chopped
Salt
Freshly ground black pepper
350 g quantity shortcrust pastry dough, made with 350 g plain flour, pinch of of salt, 175 g mixed margarine and lard and 3–4 × 15 ml spoons cold water (see page 66)
Beaten egg to glaze

Imperial

12 oz lean chuck steak, cut into $\frac{1}{2}$ inch pieces
$\frac{1}{2}$ medium onion, peeled and finely chopped
1 teaspoon dried marjoram
4 oz potato, peeled and diced
2–3 teaspoons prepared French mustard
2 oz mushrooms, finely chopped
Salt
Freshly ground black pepper
12 oz quantity shortcrust pastry dough, made with 12 oz plain flour, pinch of of salt, 6 oz mixed margarine and lard and 3–4 tablespoons cold water (see page 66)
Beaten egg to glaze

Cooking Time: $1\frac{1}{4}$ hours
Oven: 200°C, 400°F, Gas Mark 6
180°C, 350°F, Gas Mark 4

Mix together the meat, onion, marjoram, potato, mustard and mushrooms. Season well with salt and pepper. Cut the pastry dough into 4 and roll out each piece to an 18 cm (7 inch) round. Divide the filling between the rounds, piling it up in the centres. Moisten the pastry edges with water, fold each round in half and seal the edges well together. Flute the edges and glaze with beaten egg. Arrange on a baking sheet. Bake in a preheated moderately hot oven for 15 minutes, then reduce the heat to moderate and bake for a further 1 hour. Allow to cool, then pack in a rigid plastic container with an airtight lid.

Burgundy beef pies; Cornish pasties; Cumberland pie

Cumberland pie

Metric	*Imperial*
1 × 212 g packet frozen puff pastry, thawed	*1 × 7½ oz packet frozen puff pastry, thawed*
500 g pork sausagemeat	*1 lb pork sausagemeat*
2 bacon rashers, rinds removed, diced	*2 bacon rashers, rinds removed, diced*
Large pinch of dried sage or thyme	*Large pinch of dried sage or thyme*
Salt	*Salt*
Freshly ground black pepper	*Freshly ground black pepper*
4 eggs	*4 eggs*
1 × 15 ml spoon chopped fresh parsley	*1 tablespoon chopped fresh parsley*

Cooking Time: 25 to 35 minutes
Oven: 220°C, 425°F, Gas Mark 7
160°C, 325°F, Gas Mark 3

Roll out two-thirds of the dough and use to line a 20 cm (8 inch) diameter flan ring. Do not trim away the surplus dough. Cook the sausagemeat and bacon to remove excess fat. Drain and allow to cool, then place in the pastry case. Sprinkle with the sage or thyme, salt and pepper. Make four indentations in the meat and break an egg into each one. Sprinkle over the parsley. Roll out the remaining dough and dampen the edges. Use to cover the pie. Press down the edges and trim away the excess dough. Glaze with the egg white remaining in the shells. Bake in a preheated hot oven for 15 minutes, then reduce the heat to moderate and bake for a further 10 to 15 minutes. Allow to cool, then wrap in foil or carry in a rigid plastic box.

Coleslaw

Metric	Imperial
½ firm head of white cabbage, cored and thinly sliced	*½ firm head of white cabbage, cored and thinly sliced*
1 small onion, peeled and grated	*1 small onion, peeled and grated*
1 large carrot, peeled and grated	*1 large carrot, peeled and grated*
2 celery stalks, sliced	*2 celery stalks, sliced*
25 g sultanas	*1 oz sultanas*
25 g walnuts, chopped	*1 oz walnuts, chopped*
150–300 ml mayonnaise	*¼–½ pint mayonnaise*
Salt	*Salt*
Freshly ground black pepper	*Freshly ground black pepper*

Combine the cabbage, onion, carrot, celery, sultanas and walnuts in a large bowl. Stir in just enough mayonnaise to bind the mixture together. Season with salt and pepper. Place in a rigid plastic container with a tight fitting lid and chill until you leave.

Potato salad

Metric	Imperial
150 ml mayonnaise	*¼ pint mayonnaise*
Large pinch of dry mustard	*Large pinch of dry mustard*
4 spring onions, finely chopped	*4 spring onions, finely chopped*
Salt	*Salt*
Freshly ground pepper	*Freshly ground pepper*
1 kg potatoes, cooked in their skins, peeled and finely diced	*2 lb potatoes, cooked in their skins, peeled and finely diced*
2 × 15 ml spoons chopped fresh parsley	*2 tablespoons chopped fresh parsley*
Paprika	*Paprika*

Mix the mayonnaise with the mustard, spring onions and salt and pepper to taste. Add to the potatoes and stir to make sure that they are well coated. Taste and adjust the seasoning. Spoon into a rigid plastic container and sprinkle with chopped parsley and a little paprika. Keep in the refrigerator until you are ready to leave.

Roast chicken or turkey mayonnaise

Metric	Imperial
1 × 1.75–2 kg chicken or 1 × 3.5 kg turkey	*1 × 4 lb chicken or 1 × 8 lb turkey*
Tarragon Butter (see page 24)	*Tarragon Butter (see page 24)*
1 onion, peeled and halved	*1 onion, peeled and halved*
300 ml stock or water	*½ pint stock or water*
150 ml water	*¼ pint water*
150 ml dry white wine	*¼ pint dry white wine*
2 × 5 ml spoons curry powder	*2 teaspoons curry powder*
300 ml mayonnaise	*½ pint mayonnaise*
2 × 5 ml spoons whipped cream (optional)	*2 teaspoons whipped cream (optional)*

Cooking Time: Chicken – 1 hour 40 minutes
Turkey – 2½ to 3 hours
Oven: Chicken – 190°C, 375°F, Gas Mark 5
Turkey – 180°C, 350°F, Gas Mark 4

Wipe the chicken or turkey and make sure that it is completely thawed if using frozen. Place half the tarragon butter inside with half the onion. Rub the remaining butter over the bird and place in a roasting tin with the stock or water, water, wine and remainder of the onion. Roast in a preheated moderately hot or moderate oven, basting from time to time with the liquid in the tin for a really moist and delicious cold bird. Allow to cool completely before carving, then wrap in film or foil to keep moist.

Add the curry powder to the mayonnaise and mix well. For a special sauce, fold in the whipped cream. Carry this dressing in a plastic container.

Take along a Savoury Rice Salad and a plain watercress salad with chopped walnuts in separate containers.

Chicken serves 6 and turkey 8 to 10

Coleslaw; Roast chicken or turkey mayonnaise; Potato salad; Pressed ox tongue

Pressed ox tongue

Metric	*Imperial*
1 × 2 kg ox tongue, salted	*1 × 4 lb ox tongue, salted*
8 peppercorns, slightly crushed	*8 peppercorns, slightly crushed*
1 bouquet garni	*1 bouquet garni*
1 onion	*1 onion*
6 cloves	*6 cloves*

Cooking Time: About 2 to 3 hours

Soak the tongue in cold water overnight. Drain and place in a large saucepan. Cover with fresh cold water and bring to the boil. Drain and replace the tongue in the saucepan with fresh water to cover, the peppercorns, bouquet garni and the onion stuck with the cloves. Bring to the boil, cover and simmer until tender. (This can usually be judged when the skin under the tip comes away easily.) Drain the tongue, retaining 600 ml (1 pint) of the stock. Plunge the tongue into cold water and drain again. Reduce the stock to about 300 ml (½ pint) by boiling rapidly.

Place the tongue on a board and remove the skin from the tip towards the thick end, cutting off the gristle and bones. Neaten the root end by trimming. Wind into a 15–18 cm (6–7 inch) cake tin or soufflé dish, or use a small Pyrex bowl. Make sure the tongue winds round and fits snugly into the container. Pour on the reduced stock and place a plate or lid with a heavy weight on top. Leave to set. Turn out and pack in a rigid container, or leave in the tin or dish and cover with foil.

Serves 8

Virginia baked ham and Cold spiced brisket of beef in basket; Mixed salad and Savoury rice salad in bowls

Mixed salad

Metric

1 crisp lettuce, separated into leaves
4 large tomatoes, skinned and cut into 8 wedges
2 hard-boiled eggs, quartered
¼ cucumber, peeled and thinly sliced
6 spring onions
6 stuffed olives, halved

Imperial

1 crisp lettuce, separated into leaves
4 large tomatoes, skinned and cut into 8 wedges
2 hard-boiled eggs, quartered
¼ cucumber, peeled and thinly sliced
6 spring onions
6 stuffed olives, halved

Wash the lettuce leaves and pat dry with absorbent kitchen paper. Use to line a rigid plastic container. Arrange the tomatoes round the top of the lettuce alternately with the hard-boiled eggs. Arrange the cucumber in a ring below. Place the onions in a wheel shape with a centre of halved olives. Carry French Dressing in a separate container and pour over the salad at the picnic.

Virginia baked ham

Metric	Imperial
1 × 2.25 kg gammon	*1 × 5 lb gammon*
2 bay leaves	*2 bay leaves*
12 peppercorns, slightly crushed	*12 peppercorns, slightly crushed*
1 × 375 g can pineapple slices	*1 × 13 oz can pineapple slices*
2 × 15 ml spoons brown sugar	*2 tablespoons brown sugar*
Whole cloves	*Whole cloves*

Cooking Time: 2¼ hours
Oven: 200°C, 400°F, Gas Mark 6

Soak the gammon in cold water for several hours. Drain and put in a large casserole or saucepan with the bay leaves and peppercorns. Add fresh water to cover and bring to the boil, removing any scum from the surface as it forms. Simmer for 1 hour. Drain the gammon and wrap in foil. Bake in a preheated moderately hot oven for 40 minutes. Drain the pineapple and mix the juice with the brown sugar. Bring to the boil, stirring to dissolve the sugar, and boil until reduced by half. Remove the ham from the oven and peel off the skin. Score the fat into diamond shapes. Place a clove in each diamond. Put the ham in a roasting tin and pour over the brown sugar sauce, which should be thick and sticky. Place the pineapple slices over the skin. Replace the ham in the oven and bake for 20 to 25 minutes or until the skin is crisp. Allow to cool, then slice and wrap in foil.
Serves 8

Savoury rice salad

Metric	Imperial
225 g long-grain rice	*8 oz long-grain rice*
1 small bunch of spring onions, chopped	*1 small bunch of spring onions, chopped*
½ green pepper, cored, seeded and sliced	*½ green pepper, cored, seeded and sliced*
½ red pepper, cored, seeded and sliced	*½ red pepper, cored, seeded and sliced*
1 celery stalk, chopped	*1 celery stalk, chopped*
75 g cashew nuts or salted peanuts, halved	*3 oz cashew nuts or salted peanuts, halved*
Salt	*Salt*
Freshly ground black pepper	*Freshly ground black pepper*
3–4 × 15 ml spoons French Dressing (see page 23)	*3–4 tablespoons French Dressing (see page 23)*

Cook the rice in boiling salted water until tender. Drain and rinse in cold water. Drain well again. Add the spring onions, green pepper, red pepper, celery and nuts. Season well with salt and pepper and toss in the French Dressing. Put into a rigid plastic container and chill well.

Cold spiced brisket of beef

Metric	Imperial
2 kg lean boned, rolled and salted brisket	*4 lb lean boned, rolled and salted brisket*
1 small can of beer	*1 small can of beer*
1 onion, peeled and chopped	*1 onion, peeled and chopped*
1 × 5 ml spoon ground allspice	*1 teaspoon ground allspice*
1 × 5 ml spoon ground cloves	*1 teaspoon ground cloves*
1 × 5 ml spoon ground mace	*1 teaspoon ground mace*
1 × 2.5 ml spoon crushed peppercorns	*½ teaspoon crushed peppercorns*
1 × 2.5 ml spoon dried thyme	*½ teaspoon dried thyme*
1 bay leaf, crumbled	*1 bay leaf, crumbled*

Cooking Time: About 4½ hours

Put the rolled beef in a bowl and pour over the beer. Mix the onion with all the spices and herbs and rub all over the meat. Cover and leave in the refrigerator for 24 to 48 hours, turning the meat from time to time and brushing the spice mixture over all surfaces so that it penetrates.
Place the meat in a saucepan and cover with the beer and spice mixture and cold water. Bring to the boil and simmer for 4½ hours. Drain the meat and press between two plates with a weight on top. Slice when cold and wrap in foil.
Serves 6 to 8

Cherry and almond flan

Metric	*Imperial*
175 g quantity shortcrust pastry dough (see page 66)	*6 oz quantity shortcrust pastry dough (see page 66)*
50 g margarine	*2 oz margarine*
50 g caster sugar	*2 oz caster sugar*
1 egg	*1 egg*
50 g ground almonds	*2 oz ground almonds*
25 g self-raising flour	*1 oz self-raising flour*
Few drops of almond essence	*Few drops of almond essence*
1 × 450 g can cherry pie filling	*1 × 15 oz can cherry pie filling*

Cooking Time: 1 hour 20 minutes
Oven: 200°C, 400°F, Gas Mark 6

Roll out the dough and use to line a 20 cm (8 inch) loose-bottomed flan ring or a pie plate. Bake blind for 20 minutes (see page 66) and allow to cool.
Cream the margarine and sugar together and beat the egg well into the mixture. Stir in the ground almonds and sifted flour. Add the almond essence and mix well. Spread the cherry pie filling in the baked pastry case and cover with the almond mixture, spreading carefully. Bake in a preheated moderately hot oven for 35-40 minutes or until firm and golden brown. Allow to cool, then cover with cling film.
Serves 4 to 6

Cherry and almond flan; Country strawberry cream; Plum and orange tartlets; Charlotte russe

Plum and orange tartlets

Metric	*Imperial*
175 g quantity shortcrust pastry dough (see page 66)	*6 oz quantity shortcrust pastry dough (see page 66)*
225 g plums, stoned and quartered	*8 oz plums, stoned and quartered*
25 g caster sugar	*1 oz caster sugar*
Finely grated rind of ½ orange	*Finely grated rind of ½ orange*
Large pinch of ground cinnamon	*Large pinch of ground cinnamon*
2 × 5 ml spoons cornflour	*2 teaspoons cornflour*
Milk to glaze	*Milk to glaze*

Cooking Time: 25 minutes
Oven: 200°C, 400°F, Gas Mark 6

Divide the dough in half and roll out one half. Cut out four circles slightly larger than the diameter of four tartlet tins. Use to line the tins. Mix together the plums, sugar, orange rind, cinnamon and cornflour. Divide the fruit filling between the lined tins. Roll out the remaining dough and cut out four circles for lids. Moisten the edges of the dough with water. Place the lids over the fruit and press on to seal well. Brush with milk. Bake in a preheated moderately hot oven. Allow to cool, then pack in a rigid container with an airtight lid, or wrap in aluminium foil.

Charlotte russe

Metric	*Imperial*
About 16 sponge fingers	*About 16 sponge fingers*
1 × 410 g can peach slices, drained	*1 × 14½ oz can peach slices, drained*
6 egg yolks	*6 egg yolks*
50 g caster sugar	*2 oz caster sugar*
600 ml milk	*1 pint milk*
1 × 15 ml spoon powdered gelatine	*1 tablespoon powdered gelatine*
2 × 15 ml spoons water	*2 tablespoons water*
300 ml whipping cream, lightly whipped	*½ pint whipping cream, lightly whipped*
2 × 15 ml spoons peach brandy or similar liqueur	*2 tablespoons peach brandy or similar liqueur*
Pistachio nuts to decorate	*Pistachio nuts to decorate*

Line the sides of a greased 19 cm (7½ inch) diameter straight-sided soufflé dish with the sponge fingers. Trim the ends of the biscuits level with the rim of the dish. Reserve six peach slices for decoration and chop the remainder. Beat the egg yolks and sugar together until pale in colour. Warm the milk in a heavy-based saucepan. Pour onto the egg yolk mixture and return to the saucepan. Heat slowly, stirring, until the mixture coats the back of the spoon. Do not boil. Dissolve the gelatine in the water over a pan of hot water and cool slightly. Strain into the cooled custard. Mix well and chill until beginning to thicken. Fold in the cream, chopped peaches and brandy or liqueur. Spoon into the soufflé dish. Chill until set. Decorate with the reserved peach slices and pistachio nuts. Cover with foil to carry.
Serves 6

Country strawberry cream

Metric	*Imperial*
2 × 5 ml spoons powdered gelatine	*2 teaspoons powdered gelatine*
2 × 15 ml spoons water	*2 tablespoons water*
2 egg whites	*2 egg whites*
50 g caster sugar	*2 oz caster sugar*
300 ml whipping cream, lightly whipped	*½ pint whipping cream, lightly whipped*
1 × 15 ml spoon medium sherry	*1 tablespoon medium sherry*
25 g ground almonds	*1 oz ground almonds*
225 g strawberries, hulled and halved	*8 oz strawberries, hulled and halved*

Dissolve the gelatine in the water over a pan of hot water. Allow to cool slightly. Whisk the egg whites until stiff. Beat in the caster sugar until the mixture is stiff and glossy. Strain the gelatine into the cream and mix well. Fold in the sherry and almonds, then the egg white mixture and strawberries. Turn into a 2 litre (3½ pint) soufflé dish. Chill until set. Cover with foil or cling film to carry.

Chocolate squares

Metric	*Imperial*
175 g plain chocolate	*6 oz plain chocolate*
50 g margarine	*2 oz margarine*
225 g digestive biscuits	*8 oz digestive biscuits*
Grated rind of 1 orange	*Grated rind of 1 orange*
125 g sultanas	*4 oz sultanas*
50 g glacé cherries, chopped	*2 oz glacé cherries, chopped*
5 glacé cherries, halved, to decorate	*5 glacé cherries, halved, to decorate*

Melt the chocolate and margarine in a heatproof bowl over a pan of hot water. Remove from the heat. Put the biscuits in a polythene bag and crush with a rolling pin. Add to the chocolate mixture with the orange rind, sultanas and chopped cherries. Mix well and press into an 18 cm (7 inch) square tin. Mark into 9 squares and decorate with the halved cherries. Chill well before cutting into squares. Wrap the squares in foil, or carry in the tin, covered with foil.
Makes 9 squares

Nut and sultana bars

Metric	*Imperial*
100 g digestive biscuits	*4 oz digestive biscuits*
50 g plain sweet biscuits	*2 oz plain sweet biscuits*
50 g walnuts, chopped	*2 oz walnuts, chopped*
75 g sultanas	*3 oz sultanas*
2 × 15 ml spoons golden syrup	*2 tablespoons golden syrup*
75 g butter	*3 oz butter*
50 g plain chocolate	*2 oz plain chocolate*

Grease a shallow 18 cm (7 inch) square tin. Put all the biscuits in a polythene bag and crush with a rolling pin. Put into a bowl and mix in the walnuts and sultanas. Melt the golden syrup, butter and chocolate in a heatproof bowl over a pan of hot water. Pour onto the biscuit and nut mixture and mix well. Spoon into the prepared tin and smooth out with a palette knife. Chill until set, then cut into bars. Wrap the bars in foil, or carry in the tin, covered with foil.
Makes 12 bars

Spice biscuits

Metric	*Imperial*
150 g plain flour	*6 oz plain flour*
1 × 5 ml spoon ground cinnamon	*1 teaspoon ground cinnamon*
1 × 5 ml spoon ground mace	*1 teaspoon ground mace*
100 g butter	*4 oz butter*
50 g caster sugar	*2 oz caster sugar*

Cooking Time: 15 minutes
Oven: 180°C, 350°F, Gas Mark 4

Sift the flour and spices together. Cream the butter and sugar together until light and fluffy. Stir in the flour mixture and bind together with your fingertips. Roll out on a floured board to 5 mm (¼ inch) thick. Using a 6 cm (2½ inch) fluted cutter, cut out 20 rounds. Place on a greased baking sheet and prick with a fork. Bake in a preheated moderate oven for 15 minutes. Cool on a wire rack. Pack in a sealed polythene bag or carry in a rigid container with airtight lid.
Makes 20 biscuits

Ginger shortbread biscuits

Metric	*Imperial*
250 g butter, softened	*8 oz butter, softened*
125 g caster sugar	*4 oz caster sugar*
250 g plain flour	*8 oz plain flour*
2 × 5 ml spoons ground ginger	*2 teaspoons ground ginger*
Caster sugar for sprinkling	*Caster sugar for sprinkling*

Cooking Time: 15 to 20 minutes
Oven: 160°C, 325°F, Gas Mark 3

Cream together the butter and sugar on a clean surface. Gradually work in the sifted flour and ginger to form a dough. Knead until smooth. Roll out to 5 mm (¼ inch) thick and cut into rounds with a medium scone cutter, or any shaped cutter. Place on a baking sheet. Bake in a preheated moderate oven until golden brown, and sprinkle with caster sugar while still warm. When cool, wrap in foil or carry in a rigid container.

Ginger shortbread biscuits; Chocolate squares; Spice biscuits; Nut and sultana bars

SUGAR

Orange and almond gingerbread

Metric	*Imperial*
25 g flaked almonds	*1 oz flaked almonds*
350 g plain flour	*12 oz plain flour*
1 × 15 ml spoon ground ginger	*1 tablespoon ground ginger*
Finely grated rind of 1 orange	*Finely grated rind of 1 orange*
75 g margarine	*3 oz margarine*
350 g golden syrup	*12 oz golden syrup*
75 g brown sugar	*3 oz brown sugar*
Juice of 1 orange	*Juice of 1 orange*
1 egg	*1 egg*
1.5 × 5 ml spoons bicarbonate of soda	*1½ teaspoons bicarbonate of soda*

Cooking Time: 1¼ hours
Oven: 160°C, 325°F, Gas Mark 3

Sprinkle the almonds over the bottom of a greased 2 litre (3½ pint) ring mould. Sift together the flour and ginger and add the grated orange rind. Slowly heat the margarine, golden syrup, sugar and 2 × 15 ml spoons (2 tablespoons) of the orange juice together until melted and well mixed. Add to the flour mixture with the egg and beat until thoroughly mixed. Dissolve the bicarbonate of soda in the remaining orange juice and stir into the mixture. Pour into the prepared tin and bake in a preheated moderate oven until well risen and spongy. Remove from the tin and cool on a wire rack, nut side uppermost. Wrap in aluminium foil, or pack in a plastic container with an airtight lid.

Old world plum cake

Metric	*Imperial*
200 g soft margarine	*8 oz soft margarine*
200 g caster sugar	*8 oz caster sugar*
4 standard eggs	*4 large eggs*
Finely grated rind of 1 lemon	*Finely grated rind of 1 lemon*
100 g self-raising flour	*4 oz self-raising flour*
100 g plain flour	*4 oz plain flour*
1 × 15 ml spoon medium sherry	*1 tablespoon medium sherry*
1 × 410 g can prunes, drained, stoned and roughly chopped	*1 × 14½ oz can prunes, drained, stoned and roughly chopped*
50 g ground almonds	*2 oz ground almonds*
50 g walnuts, roughly chopped	*2 oz walnuts, roughly chopped*

Cooking Time: 2 to 2¼ hours
Oven: 150°C, 300°F, Gas Mark 2

Grease and line an 18 cm (7 inch) square cake tin. Cream the margarine and sugar together until light and fluffy. Beat in the eggs, one at a time. Stir in the lemon rind, sifted flours and sherry. Fold in the prunes, ground almonds and walnuts. Spoon into the prepared tin and bake in a preheated cool oven for 2 to 2¼ hours. Turn out and cool on a wire rack. Wrap in foil, or carry in the tin, covered with cling film.

Banana and honey cake

Metric	*Imperial*
350 g self-raising flour	*12 oz self-raising flour*
1 × 2.5 ml spoon ground mace	*½ teaspoon ground mace*
150 g soft margarine	*6 oz soft margarine*
150 g caster sugar	*6 oz caster sugar*
3 standard eggs	*3 standard eggs*
3 × 15 ml spoons clear honey	*3 tablespoons clear honey*
2 bananas, peeled and mashed	*2 bananas, peeled and mashed*
200 g sultanas	*8 oz sultanas*
100 g glacé cherries, quartered	*4 oz glacé cherries, quartered*
100 g hazelnuts, roughly chopped	*4 oz hazelnuts, roughly chopped*

Cooking Time: 2 hours
Oven: 180°C, 350°F, Gas Mark 4
150°C, 300°F, Gas Mark 2

Grease and line a 24 cm (9½ inch) spring-release cake tin (2.25 litre/4 pint capacity). Sift the flour and mace together. Cream the margarine and sugar together until light and fluffy. Beat in the eggs, one at a time. Fold the flour into the mixture, alternating with the honey and mashed bananas. Stir in the sultanas, glacé cherries and hazelnuts. Spoon into the prepared tin. Bake in a preheated moderate oven for 1 hour, then reduce the heat to cool and bake for a further 1 hour. Allow to cool slightly then turn out onto a wire rack to cool completely. Wrap in foil or carry in the tin, covered with cling film.

Old world plum cake; Orange and almond gingerbread; Banana and honey cake

Wholemeal bread

Metric	Imperial
450 g wholemeal flour	*1 lb wholemeal flour*
450 g strong plain flour	*1 lb strong plain flour*
2 × 5 ml spoons salt	*2 teaspoons salt*
25 g lard	*1 oz lard*
25 g fresh yeast or	*1 oz fresh yeast or*
5 × 5 ml spoons dried yeast	*5 teaspoons dried yeast*
3 × 5 ml spoons sugar	*3 teaspoons sugar*
600 ml warm water	*1 pint warm water*

Cooking Time: About 15 to 20 minutes
Oven: 230°C, 450°F, Gas Mark 8

Sift the flours and salt into a bowl and rub in the lard. Mix the fresh yeast with the sugar and dissolve in 150 ml (¼ pint) of the water, or dissolve the sugar in the water and sprinkle on the dried yeast. Leave for 10 minutes or until frothy. Make a well in the centre of the flour and add the yeast mixture and remaining water. Form into a dough and knead on a lightly floured board for 10 minutes or until smooth and elastic. Place in a lightly oiled polythene bag or in a covered bowl and leave to rise until doubled in size.
Turn out onto a lightly floured board and knead for about 2 minutes. Divide into two and shape into rounds. Place on baking sheets and cut a cross in the tops. Leave to rise, covered, for a further 20 minutes. Bake in a preheated hot oven until golden brown and sounding hollow when tapped on the bottoms. Wrap in foil or place in a polythene bag. Take butter in a separate rigid plastic container.
Makes 2 loaves

Bap rolls

Metric	Imperial
350 g plain flour	*12 oz plain flour*
1 × 2.5 ml spoon salt	*½ teaspoon salt*
40 g lard	*1½ oz lard*
15 g fresh yeast or 2.5 × 5 ml spoons dried yeast	*½ oz fresh yeast or 2½ teaspoons dried yeast*
1 × 5 ml spoon sugar	*1 teaspoon sugar*
Scant 300 ml mixed milk and water	*Scant ½ pint mixed milk and water*

Cooking Time: About 15 minutes
Oven: 230°C, 450°F, Gas Mark 8

Sift the flour and salt into a bowl and rub in the lard. Mix the fresh yeast with the sugar and dissolve in the milk and water mixture, or dissolve the sugar in the milk and water and sprinkle on the dried yeast. Leave until frothy.
Make a well in the centre of the flour and add the yeast mixture. Form into a dough and knead on a lightly floured board for 10 minutes or until smooth and elastic. Place in a lightly oiled polythene bag or in a covered bowl and leave to rise until double in size. (Quick Rise – 45 to 60 minutes in a warm place. Slower Rise – 2 hours at average room temperature. Cold Rise – 12 to 24 hours in a refrigerator.)
Turn out onto a lightly floured board and knead for about 2 minutes. Form into 10 small ovals and place on a greased baking sheet. Brush the baps with milk, dust with flour and allow to rise for a further 15 to 20 minutes. Dust again with flour and press the tops down with the palm of the hand. Bake in a preheated hot oven.
Makes 10

Cherry cake

Metric	Imperial
250 g glacé cherries, halved, washed and dried	*8 oz glacé cherries, halved, washed and dried*
125 g self-raising flour	*4 oz self-raising flour*
75 g plain flour	*3 oz plain flour*
25 g cornflour	*1 oz cornflour*
175 g soft margarine	*6 oz soft margarine*
175 g caster sugar	*6 oz caster sugar*
3 standard eggs	*3 standard eggs*
Finely grated rind of 1 lemon	*Finely grated rind of 1 lemon*
25 g nibbed almonds	*1 oz nibbed almonds*

Cooking Time: 1¼ hours
Oven: 180°C, 350°F, Gas Mark 4

Grease and line an 18 cm (7 inch) round cake tin. Put the cherries and 25 g (1 oz) of the self-raising flour in a polythene bag and toss to coat the cherries. (This will prevent them sinking in the cake.) Sift the remaining flours and cornflour into a bowl. Cream the margarine and sugar together until light and fluffy. Beat in the eggs, one at a time. Stir in the sifted flours, lemon rind, nibbed almonds and cherries. Spoon into the prepared tin and bake in a preheated moderate oven until well risen and golden. Turn out and cool on a wire rack. Wrap in foil or carry in the tin, covered with cling film.

Cherry cake; Picnic fruit cake; Wholemeal bread; Bap rolls

Picnic fruit cake

Metric	*Imperial*
100 g soft margarine	*4 oz soft margarine*
150 g caster sugar	*6 oz caster sugar*
3 standard eggs	*3 large eggs*
150 g self-raising flour	*6 oz self-raising flour*
100 g seedless raisins	*4 oz seedless raisins*
50 g glacé cherries, quartered	*2 oz glacé cherries, quartered*
50 g mixed candied peel	*2 oz mixed candied peel*
100 g sultanas	*4 oz sultanas*
1 × 5 ml spoon almond essence	*1 teaspoon almond essence*
25 g soft brown sugar	*1 oz soft brown sugar*

Cooking Time: 1 hour
Oven: 180°C, 350°F, Gas Mark 4

Line a 28 × 18 × 3 cm (11 × 7 × $1\frac{1}{4}$ inch) tin with greaseproof paper. Cream the margarine and sugar together until light and fluffy. Beat in the eggs, one at a time. Sift in the flour and stir in with a metal spoon. Mix in the fruit and almond essence. Spoon into the tin and level out the mixture. Sprinkle over the brown sugar. Bake in the centre of a preheated moderate oven until risen and golden brown. Turn out onto a wire rack. Allow to cool then cut into bars. Wrap in foil or cling film.
Makes 16 bars

Sandwich fillings

Sandwiches must be made very carefully for picnics if they are not to end up limp and sad. It is often a good idea to take several different fillings in plastic boxes and leave people to make their own sandwiches on the spot. For this type of picnic take several kinds of bread and rolls, wrapped in foil to keep them fresh, and a selection of salad ingredients in a plastic box.

When preparing sandwiches, always spread butter or fillings all over the bread, otherwise they will have dry, unappetizing edges. Use the savoury butters (pages 24 and 25) to add extra flavour to meat fillings.

Sandwiches can be prepared in advance and frozen if a suitable filling is used, for example meat, tuna fish, salmon, etc., but beware of wet fillings such as tomatoes or cucumber which make for soggy sandwiches. Allow 4 to 5 hours for defrosting.

Cottage cheese and chive filling

Metric	*Imperial*
50 g butter, softened	*2 oz butter, softened*
125 g cottage cheese	*4 oz cottage cheese*
1 × 5 ml spoon chopped fresh chives	*1 teaspoon chopped fresh chives*

Cream the butter, cottage cheese and chives thoroughly together and chill before using.
Fills 4 sandwiches

Hard-boiled egg filling

Metric	*Imperial*
1 hard-boiled egg, very finely chopped	*1 hard-boiled egg, very finely chopped*
25 g butter, softened	*1 oz butter, softened*
1 × 15 ml spoon mayonnaise	*1 tablespoon mayonnaise*
Salt	*Salt*
Freshly ground pepper	*Freshly ground pepper*

Add the hard-boiled egg to the butter and mix well. Stir in the mayonnaise with salt and pepper to taste.
Fills 3 sandwiches

Ham and tomato filling

Metric	*Imperial*
1 slice of cooked ham, finely chopped	*1 slice of cooked ham, finely chopped*
1 tomato, skinned and finely chopped	*1 tomato, skinned and finely chopped*
50 g butter, softened	*2 oz butter, softened*
Salt	*Salt*
Freshly ground pepper	*Freshly ground pepper*

Mix together the ham, tomato and butter and season to taste with salt and pepper.
Fills 2 sandwiches

Sandwich fillings: Cottage cheese and chive; Hard-boiled egg; Ham and tomato

Chicken filling

Metric	*Imperial*
125 g cooked chicken, minced	*4 oz cooked chicken, minced*
1 slice of cooked ham, finely chopped	*1 slice of cooked ham, finely chopped*
Pinch of paprika	*Pinch of paprika*
50 g butter, softened	*2 oz butter, softened*
2 × 15 ml spoons mayonnaise	*2 tablespoons mayonnaise*
Salt	*Salt*
Freshly ground pepper	*Freshly ground pepper*

Mix together the chicken, ham and paprika. Beat in the butter, then add the mayonnaise with salt and pepper to taste.
Fills 4 sandwiches

Tuna and tomato filling

Metric	*Imperial*
1 × 200 g can tuna fish, drained and flaked	*1 × 7 oz can tuna fish, drained and flaked*
2 × 5 ml spoons vinegar	*2 teaspoons vinegar*
2 × 15 ml spoons tomato ketchup	*2 tablespoons tomato ketchup*
2 tomatoes, skinned and finely chopped	*2 tomatoes, skinned and finely chopped*
Salt	*Salt*
Freshly ground pepper	*Freshly ground pepper*
50 g butter, softened	*2 oz butter, softened*

Mix together the tuna fish, vinegar, tomato ketchup and tomatoes. Add salt and pepper to taste, then combine with the butter.
Fills 6 sandwiches

Corned beef and chutney filling

Metric	*Imperial*
50 g butter, softened	*2 oz butter, softened*
1 × 200 g can corned beef, drained and mashed	*1 × 7 oz can corned beef, drained and mashed*
2 × 15 ml spoons chutney	*2 tablespoons chutney*
Salt	*Salt*
Freshly ground pepper	*Freshly ground pepper*

Beat together the butter and corned beef. Add the chutney with salt and pepper to taste and mix well.
Alternatively, spread the bread with Mustard Butter, then spread with mashed corned beef.
Fills 4 to 6 sandwiches

Sandwich fillings: Cress butter; Chicken; Corned beef and chutney; Tuna and tomato; Cucumber and celery

Cucumber and celery filling

Metric	*Imperial*
50 g butter, softened	*2 oz butter, softened*
2.5 cm piece cucumber, peeled and very finely chopped	*1 inch piece cucumber, peeled and very finely chopped*
1 small celery stalk, very finely chopped	*1 small celery stalk, very finely chopped*
Salt	*Salt*
Freshly ground pepper	*Freshly ground pepper*

Beat together the butter, cucumber and celery. Add salt and pepper to taste and mix well.
Fills 3 sandwiches

Cress butter filling

Metric	*Imperial*
50 g butter, softened	*2 oz butter, softened*
½ carton mustard and cress, washed and dried	*½ carton mustard and cress, washed and dried*
Salt	*Salt*
Freshly ground pepper	*Freshly ground pepper*
1 × 2.5 ml spoon dry mustard	*½ teaspoon dry mustard*

Beat together the butter and cress. Add salt and pepper to taste and the mustard and mix well.
Fills 2 to 3 sandwiches

Cheese and sausage pinwheels

Metric	*Imperial*
6 slices of white bread, cut lengthways from an uncut loaf, crusts removed	*6 slices of white bread, cut lengthways from an uncut loaf, crusts removed*
1 × 15 ml spoon tomato ketchup	*1 tablespoon tomato ketchup*
175 g cream cheese	*6 oz cream cheese*
1 × 5 ml spoon chopped fresh chives	*1 teaspoon chopped fresh chives*
Salt	*Salt*
Freshly ground pepper	*Freshly ground pepper*
6 skinless sausages, cooked	*6 skinless sausages, cooked*

Roll out the bread slices with a rolling pin to flatten them. Mix together the tomato ketchup, cream cheese, chives and salt and pepper to taste. Spread on the bread. Place a sausage at one edge of each slice and roll up. Wrap the rolls in foil and chill for 30 minutes before cutting into slices. Carry in a rigid plastic container or wrapped in foil.

Picnic layer loaf

Metric	*Imperial*
1 small wholemeal loaf, unsliced	*1 small wholemeal loaf, unsliced*
Cottage Cheese and Chive Filling (see page 87)	*Cottage Cheese and Chive Filling (see page 87)*
Hard-boiled Egg Filling (see page 87)	*Hard-boiled Egg Filling (see page 87)*
Ham and Tomato Filling (see page 87)	*Ham and Tomato Filling (see page 87)*
Cress Butter Filling (see page 89)	*Cress Butter Filling (see page 89)*
Cucumber and Celery Filling (see page 89)	*Cucumber and Celery Filling (see page 89)*
225 g cream cheese	*8 oz cream cheese*
75 g peanuts, crushed	*3 oz peanuts, crushed*

Remove the crust from the top and bottom of the loaf, then slice lengthways into 6 slices. Spread five slices with a filling, the ham and tomato filling in the centre, then put the loaf together again and cover with the remaining slice. Press well down. Wrap in foil and chill for at least 1 hour. Remove the crusts from the sides of the loaf with a sharp bread knife. Spread the sides with the cream cheese. Press the peanuts onto the sides and top. Wrap in foil again and cut into slices at the picnic.

Serves 6

NOTE: This loaf can be frozen successfully. Allow 4 to 5 hours thawing time.

French picnic bread

Metric	*Imperial*
1 French loaf	*1 French loaf*
½ quantity Cress Butter Filling (see page 89)	*½ quantity Cress Butter Filling (see page 89)*
Corned Beef and Chutney Filling (see page 88)	*Corned Beef and Chutney Filling (see page 88)*
½ quantity Mustard Butter (see page 25)	*½ quantity Mustard Butter (see page 25)*
2 tomatoes, skinned and sliced	*2 tomatoes, skinned and sliced*
2 hard-boiled eggs, sliced	*2 hard-boiled eggs, sliced*

Cut the French bread into 4 slices lengthways, not cutting all the way through. Spread the top slice with the Cress Butter, the second with the Corned Beef and Chutney Filling and the third with the Mustard Butter. Add the sliced tomatoes and hard-boiled eggs to the third layer. Wrap in foil and slice with a sharp knife immediately before serving.

Picnic layer loaf; Cheese and sausage pinwheels; French picnic bread

BARBECUE AND PICNIC DRINKS

Sangria

Metric	*Imperial*
600 ml red wine	*1 pint red wine*
4 × 15 ml spoons brandy	*4 tablespoons brandy*
150 ml orange juice	*$\frac{1}{4}$ pint orange juice*
600 ml lemonade	*1 pint lemonade*
1 orange, thinly sliced	*1 orange, thinly sliced*
1 lemon, thinly sliced	*1 lemon, thinly sliced*
1 apple, cored and thinly sliced	*1 apple, cored and thinly sliced*
Ice cubes	*Ice cubes*

Mix the red wine and brandy in a large jug or bowl. Add the orange juice, strained if fresh, and lemonade and stir well. Float slices of fruit in the mixture with the ice cubes.
Serves 8

Citrus cooler

Metric	*Imperial*
1 × 178 ml can frozen concentrated orange juice, thawed	*1 × $6\frac{1}{4}$ fl oz can frozen concentrated orange juice, thawed*
1 × 178 ml can frozen concentrated grapefruit juice, thawed	*1 × $6\frac{1}{4}$ fl oz can frozen concentrated grapefruit juice, thawed*
300 ml water	*$\frac{1}{2}$ pint water*
Ice cubes	*Ice cubes*
1 orange, sliced	*1 orange, sliced*
1 lemon, sliced	*1 lemon, sliced*
Soda water	*Soda water*

Combine the fruit juices with the water in a jug. Put ice cubes in 8 tumblers with the orange and lemon slices. Divide the fruit juice mixture between the glasses and top up with soda water.
This cooling summer drink looks attractive served in tall glasses with the rims generously dampened and dipped in granulated sugar.

Sangria; White wine cooler; Citrus cooler; Iced white coffee

White wine cooler

Metric	*Imperial*
Crushed ice	*Crushed ice*
1 orange	*1 orange*
1 lemon	*1 lemon*
1 bottle dry white wine	*1 bottle dry white wine*
Soda water	*Soda water*

Ice is easily crushed by placing in a polythene bag and hitting with a hammer. Place the crushed ice in tall glasses. Take thin slices of rind from the orange and lemon and place on the ice. Slice the lemon into 8 slices and place on the ice. Pour in the wine and fill the glasses with soda water.
Serves 8

Minted iced tea

Metric	*Imperial*
1 lemon, finely chopped	*1 lemon, finely chopped*
1 × 15 ml spoon sugar	*1 tablespoon sugar*
8 fresh mint sprigs	*8 fresh mint sprigs*
1.2 litres weak tea, strained	*2 pints weak tea, strained*
4–8 halved lemon slices, to garnish	*4–8 halved lemon slices, to garnish*

Put the lemon in the bottom of a jug with the sugar and 4 of the mint sprigs, chopped. Pour on the tea. Allow the mixture to infuse for 20 to 30 minutes then strain into a suitable container for the picnic. Chill well. To serve, decorate each glass with a sprig of mint and a halved lemon slice.
Serves 4 to 8

Iced black coffee

Metric	*Imperial*
1.2 litres strong black coffee	*2 pints strong black coffee*

Pour 600 ml (1 pint) of the coffee into ice cube trays and freeze until solid. Chill the remaining coffee in a covered earthenware or glass container in the refrigerator. Chill for 1 to 2 hours. For a picnic, carry the ice cubes in a thermos flask. Serve by pouring the coffee over the coffee ice cubes. Milk and sugar may be added to taste, but unsweetened black coffee is the most refreshing.

Iced white coffee

Metric	*Imperial*
600 ml milk	*1 pint milk*
2 × 15 ml spoons instant coffee powder	*2 tablespoons instant coffee powder*
25 g sugar	*1 oz sugar*
300 ml cold water	*½ pint cold water*
150 ml whipped cream	*¼ pint whipped cream*

Heat the milk and whisk in the coffee and sugar. When the sugar has dissolved, add the cold water. Allow to cool, then chill well. Pour the mixture into glasses over coffee ice cubes (see above). Decorate with spoonfuls of whipped cream.

Iced black coffee; Minted iced tea

Fruit punch; Champagne fizz punch; Lemonade; Spicy mulled cider; Guy Fawkes' punch

Fruit punch

Metric	*Imperial*
300 ml sugar syrup (see Lemonade opposite), cooled	*½ pint sugar syrup (see Lemonade opposite), cooled*
300 ml orange juice, chilled	*½ pint orange juice, chilled*
300 ml pineapple juice, chilled	*½ pint pineapple juice, chilled*
600 ml weak cold tea, strained	*1 pint weak cold tea, strained*
Sliced fruit (orange, lemon, apple and pineapple as available)	*Sliced fruit (orange, lemon, apple and pineapple as available)*
Crushed ice	*Crushed ice*
Fresh mint sprigs	*Fresh mint sprigs*
300 ml ginger ale	*½ pint ginger ale*

Pour the sugar syrup into a jug and stir in the fruit juices and tea. Add sliced fruit with the crushed ice. Pour into glasses and decorate each with a mint sprig. Top up with ginger ale.
Serves 8 to 10

Spiced mulled cider

Metric	*Imperial*
2 × 15 ml spoons soft brown sugar	*2 tablespoons soft brown sugar*
Pinch of salt	*Pinch of salt*
2.25 litres dry cider	*4 pints dry cider*
1 × 5 ml spoon whole allspice berries	*1 teaspoon whole allspice berries*
Large pinch of grated nutmeg	*Large pinch of grated nutmeg*
5 cm cinnamon stick	*2 inch cinnamon stick*
1 orange	*1 orange*

Mix the brown sugar, salt and cider together in a saucepan. Place the allspice and nutmeg in a square of muslin, tie into a small package and add to the cider with the cinnamon stick. Bring slowly to just under boiling point. Add twists of orange rind and a slice of orange when serving.
Serves 8 to 10

Guy Fawkes' punch

Metric	*Imperial*
2 × 15 ml spoons brandy	*2 tablespoons brandy*
1 × 425 g can apricot slices	*1 × 15 oz can apricot slices*
1 litre red wine	*1 litre red wine*
2 × 15 ml spoons dry sherry	*2 tablespoons dry sherry*
3 × 15 ml spoons port	*3 tablespoons port*
300 ml water	*½ pint water*
1 cinnamon stick	*1 cinnamon stick*
12 cloves	*12 cloves*

Mix together the brandy and apricot slices, with the can juice. Put the wine, sherry, port, water, cinnamon and cloves in a saucepan and bring slowly to the boil. Add the fruit mixture and serve hot.

Lemonade

Metric	*Imperial*
250 g sugar	*8 oz sugar*
600 ml water	*1 pint water*
2 × 15 ml spoons lemon juice per glass	*2 tablespoons lemon juice per glass*
Ice cubes	*Ice cubes*
Soda water or water	*Soda water or water*
Fresh mint sprigs	*Fresh mint sprigs*
Lemon slices	*Lemon slices*

Put the sugar and water in a saucepan and stir to dissolve over a low heat. Allow to cool and use this as a base for lemonade drinks. Place 3 to 4 × 15 ml spoons (3 to 4 tablespoons) of the sugar syrup in a tall glass with the lemon juice. Add ice cubes and fill the glass with soda water, or water if a still drink is preferred. Decorate with a sprig of mint and a slice of lemon.

Champagne fizz punch

Metric	*Imperial*
1 fresh pineapple, peeled, cored and finely chopped	*1 fresh pineapple, peeled, cored and finely chopped*
100 g caster sugar	*4 oz caster sugar*
300 ml lemon juice	*½ pint lemon juice*
1 jar Maraschino cherries, drained	*1 jar Maraschino cherries, drained*
4 × 15 ml spoons orange-flavoured liqueur	*4 tablespoons orange-flavoured liqueur*
150 ml brandy	*¼ pint brandy*
150 ml rum (optional)	*¼ pint rum (optional)*
2–3 bottles sparkling white wine	*2–3 bottles sparkling white wine*

Put the pineapple in the bottom of a punch bowl. Sprinkle with the sugar. Allow to soak for 2 hours. Add the lemon juice, cherries, orange-flavoured liqueur, brandy and rum, if using. Mix thoroughly and allow to stand for another 12 hours. Just before serving, place a large block of ice (in preference to ice cubes) in the centre of the punch bowl and pour in the sparkling wine.
Serves about 25 to 30

Index